Gracefully

A Journey of Self-Discovery

By Alicia R. Stokes
and
Tyeisha L. Dalton

Copyright © 2020 By Alicia R. Stokes and Tyeisha L. Dalton.

All rights reserved. No part of this publication may be reproduced, distributed, or transmitted in any form or by any means, including photocopying, recording, or other electronic or mechanical methods, without the prior written permission of the publisher, except in the case of brief quotations embodied in critical reviews and certain other noncommercial uses permitted by copyright law. For permission requests, write to the publisher, addressed "Attention: Permissions Coordinator," at the address below.

ISBN: 978-0-578-63436-4 (Paperback)

Any references to historical events, real people, or real places are used fictitiously. Names, characters, and places are products of the author's imagination.

Front cover image by James Vance, Advanced Pixels.

Book design by James Vance, Advanced Pixels.

Printed by McNaughton & Gunn., in the United States of America.

First printing edition 2020.

Acknowledgments

We, Alicia and Tyeisha would like to give a special thanks to our contributors Christine Dalton, Kimberly Norris, Cecelia Wilson, Shari Ivery, Stephanie Brown, and Denise Arnold, for their amazing testimonials. We would like to thank James Vance and Advance Pixels for the beautiful book cover. A special thank you to Christon' Valle, our second editor, for his passion and care for the work. Latoya Smith, thank you for forcing us to be more vulnerable as you helped sculpt our work early on. Danielle Marcus, Tyeisha's cousin, and esteemed author thank you for your wisdom and sharing openly from your knowledge bank throughout our writing journey. Denise Rabi, what a beautiful addition as final editior. You stepped in, in the the last hour and we are eternally grateful to you. You taking your time loving on our project to get us to the finish line. Much love!

I first want to acknowledge my creator for genuinely giving me peace that surpasses all understanding. Writing this book and pouring out my heart was no easy task. Thank you for being with me all along, for never forsaking me. Thank you, God, for giving me the courage to share my story while in the midst of a storm. Thank you for showing me countless times that I am wonderfully and beautifully made and will always be more than enough.

To Isaac, my husband, thank you for loving me. Our marriage allowed me to be introduced to God and come to experience love from him in a way that has been foreign to me for many years. Thanks for your support along this journey.

To Gwendolyn Smith, my best friend, and mother. I thank you for all the love and prayers you have shared with me. This has been quite a journey, but I know your prayers have shielded and protected me. There is no greater love. I write this book in honor of you.

To my angels here on earth Isaac and Ivy. One day you will read this book and I hope that you will both be healthy, healed and whole. I pray that you are living confidently as the individual God has called you to be. When storms arise, because they will, I pray that I have shown you how to go to God with your issues and trust and believe that all things will work together for your good. I dedicate this book to both of you. I love you.

To my earthly sisters thank you for your love and support I would have never been able to be as vulnerable as I was in this book without your prayers, encouragement, and support. I love you all.

-Alicia Stokes

Preface

Two women, Two Stories: Back Story

Alicia and Tyeisha met four years ago on Facebook. A simple post in an employment group sparked a friendship and partnership creating No Ordinary Girl and this book, Gracefully Broken: A Journey of Self Discovery. No Ordinary Girl is a non-profit designed to identify generational curses in women and young girls providing tools to eliminate them. The goal is to promote healthy living, positive body image, continued education, family planning, and career coaching. As Alicia and Tyeisha began doing business, they forged a bond, a sisterhood. Alicia completed a resume for Tyeisha, which assisted in securing gainful employment after a small stint of unemployment, and from there, Tyeisha began referring people to Alicia for resume and employment services.

Alicia and Tyeisha came together again in 2017, to give back to the community through Brand You Staffing's Career Empowerment Fair. The event was a huge success, and shortly after, Tyeisha approached Alicia and another young woman to complete a book for single mothers. The book would share the stories and journeys of a mother through marriage, singleness, and divorce. As the writing commenced, the concept developed into two women sharing their journey's navigating from girls into womanhood and motherhood.

Alicia and Tyeisha have left it all on these pages, sit down, get comfortable, and prepare to be empowered by the stories of strength, endurance, and the power felt in rising from the ashes!

Part 1

Introduction

AS A LITTLE GIRL, I remember having my whole life planned out. I knew what my wedding would look like, how many children I would have, what kind of car I would drive and so on and so forth. I remember playing "house" as we would call it with my best friend and cousin; at such a tender age, everything made perfect sense. As an innocent child, you never fully understand the implications of living or the trials and tribulations that are promised to all of us. It's been such a battle to let go of what I think my life should look like.

My entire identity has been defined by what I thought it should look like, yet it had to be approved by my loved ones. Up until recently, I cannot recall a time where I decided for myself without consulting with someone else. I've spent far too long consulting with my significant other, my parents, my friends, and absurdly enough never went to God. It wasn't about living for God or even fear. It was about getting the approval of my loved ones. I indeed lacked the confidence to decide for myself. If they didn't approve, I closed the door without a second thought. Their approval meant more to me than my own happiness. It was difficult making the decision to write this book. I second-guessed myself, even quit writing because Satan's voice was bigger than my own. It took for me to lose to win again. To the world I was winning and to keep up that front, I sacrificed myself—what a costly lesson. Now, I am picking up the pieces to my shattered fairytale but this time I'm building my foundation with God. I remember tweeting years ago that I bend, I don't break. I lied. I've been broken yet saved by His grace. I am Gracefully Broken!

I've learned simply from living and facing some pretty difficult trials that the manuscript for living is God's word alone. As I turned the pages to His word, I find solace in knowing that every battle I've faced, every time my heart shattered, every puddle-filled tear, if given to God, will be used for good. As you turn the pages of our stories, I'm sure at some point you'll be able to pinpoint a time in your life when the fairytale you had all planned out has been plagued with some of the most beautiful moments yet equally intertwined with pain. I can assure you every seemingly endless battle, every broken heart, every weeping moment, serves a purpose.

Isaiah 66:9 "In the same way I will not cause pain without allowing something new to be born, If I cause you the pain, I will not stop you from giving birth to your new nation, "says your God." NCV

Chapter One

Daddy's Home

I VIVIDLY REMEMBER WAITING by the back steps every single night anticipating and awaiting the arrival of my father after he finished his shift. I can still hear the laughter and feel the embrace soon after he walked through the door repetitiously every single night. He usually greeted me singing *My Girl* by the Temptations and he knew just what to say to keep me giggling all night. I can still hear the love in his voice singing "My Girl, My Girl, My Girl, I'm talking about my girl." It's ironic because usually, the thought of this moment would bring a ray of sunshine all over my face.

As I write these words, tears are literally spilling down my cheeks, and if I had to use one word to describe how I felt, it would be empty. The very thing that used to light up my world now brings a feeling of longing and emptiness, feelings I strategically suppressed for over twenty years. I often find myself staring into the eyes of complete strangers, hoping to find any spec of pain resembling the little girl who I lost so long ago. If I can relate to just one other person, then I would know that I am not alone. Solitude and idle thoughts filled with suppressed pain and empty tears have a way of eating at your self-esteem, often leaving you void, emotionless and with thoughts of unworthiness.

My dad was there for all my first moments and he always made it such a big deal. His deep voice was so intriguing and filled with so much love, so much charisma. Now that I think about it, his presence mattered more to me than my accomplishments, milestones I encountered or heartbreaks I faced. Others might describe my dad as quiet and reserved but he was never that way with me; he possessed an extreme character that even in my darkest moments he could say one thing and I knew without a doubt I would be okay. It's something special about parents' interactions with their children. To the world, he was just an ordinary man, but he was my protector, my provider, my safe place, my hero, my superman, my first true love.

It's every girl's dream to have the bond my father and I shared. His presence made me feel so alive; his voice could calm a war and his hugs assured me I was his princess and I pretty much ruled our house. I had him wrapped around my finger and there was literally nothing I could not have when Daddy was involved. Somehow early on, life had a way of disturbing the love and bond I shared with my daddy. It came like a thief in the night, stripping everything I had known for the last several years. I lost my dad—not to death, nor absence or any fault of his own but to sin; a sin he didn't commit, nor should he pay for, but he did. A sin so great my innocence was stripped changing the dynamic of our relationship in such a daunting manner. I was forced to carry a burden I was not equipped to carry, yet I was too afraid to give it to the only man who was strong enough to carry my burdens. I was heartbroken and alone in my own home and no one knew it but me.

After my uncle took my innocence and I became a woman at the tender age of seven, I decided I no longer needed him to be my superhero. I'd just take on the role myself. My parents needed protection from my truth because if they found out, they'd surely look at me differently. Molestation scars you and leaves you feeling unwanted, dirty and unworthy. I had to protect what good was left in me, so I was determined to be everything my parents wanted me to be. I knew eventually if I did what they said, maintained good grades and kept up with my chores, it would be enough to make them see beyond the happy little girl I pretended to be. See, I was conditioned to believe at the mere age of 7, my worth was based on the approval of others and what I could give them without any expectation of reciprocity. Surely, they would eventually learn to measure my love based on what I did, not who I was. Besides, his sin made me despise who I was, so I was fine with being anyone other than my true authentic self.

I quickly learned the art and finesse of the facade. I was so good at pretending that I truly forgot who I was. In middle school, I attended a small parochial school filled with faces that looked nothing like mine. I hated it, as I was one of the only black girls in a school full of privileged white children. Kids that couldn't possibly understand the burden of being a black child with wounds. I told myself time and time again, "Alicia, your parents pay a lot of money for you to be here, do what you have to do to make them proud. Don't mess this up." To survive that experience, I had no choice but to become my classmates. I mirrored their very existence; I began to talk like them, style my hair like them, even walk like them; they seemed so happy. I pretended my way through school, through life, in my neighborhood. Even in my own home, the facade was the Band-Aid that covered up my wounds..... covering up my wounds.

I wanted so badly for my dad to see the invisible Band-Aid I had placed on my uncle's sin, but he didn't. How could he? Didn't he notice the change in me? Why didn't he ask? I was filled with rage, anger, and sadness and I hated myself because I couldn't tell my truth. Fear of telling the truth would have impacted and possibly destroyed our family dynamic so my silence, in my mind and opinion saved them and continued to uphold peace.

I witnessed many neighborhood children live in broken homes with absent fathers and pain-filled mothers, I couldn't possibly begin to fathom the damage his sin would cause. If only I knew and understood the magnitude of the damage, I would self-inflict by withholding his sin, maybe I would have been more open to ripping off that damn Band-Aid. But at the time the greatest good was protecting my family. The molestation was sporadic yet lasted for years. Plagued with alcohol abuse and generational curses this has unfortunately been swept under rugs for years. The rugs were the cover-up and alcohol abuse the medicine suppressing the painful secrets. These secrets have haunted and scarred the men and women in our family for generations. A curse my abuser, my uncle, ended up taking with him to his grave. Watching my grandmother and mother mourn his death was conflicting, I simply didn't know how to feel. Seeing them hurt as I harbored feelings of relief was too big of a burden for any child to carry but I did, and I've endured so much pain. I've always been a great writer and speaker so when my family suggested that I write a poem and read it at my abuser's funeral I obliged. I would do anything to feel valued and worthy, to make my family happy. Even if that meant standing before a lifeless monster that took my innocence. I felt disgusted, ashamed and broken as I declared how much I would miss him and how great a loss his death was to our family. His death was a beginning to an end. The molestation ended but the trauma was only the beginning.

John 16:33 "In this world you will have trouble. But take heart I have overcome the world. (NIV)

Alicia R. Stokes & Tyeisha L. Dalton

Dear Daddy

Daddy, our recent talks in our most vulnerable moments confirm you did the best you could with the information you were given to protect and love me in the way only a father can. I look back over my life and realize that Eric and I were your number one priority and our happiness seemingly always outweighed your own. Although I have never had transparent talks with you about your upbringing from the stories Mommy shared with me, I am in love with the father you are, considering the things you have been through.

Your actions always proved we were important, and your love triumphed over anything we have ever been through. I now know that had I shared with you what I endured; you would've done everything in your power to protect me. For the fear of disappointing you, as to me you embodied perfection, I kept painful secrets to protect you and caused myself so much pain, but there is beauty in the ashes.

See, had I not gone through those things, I would not be the woman, wife, and mother I am today. I'm sharing my story, not in an attempt to hurt nor shame you, I am sharing my story to help those with similar stories, to realize that broken crayons still color and God can turn our deepest pain into our biggest testimony. I now understand you were truly the best parent you knew how to be, and no one can ever take that away from you.

Writing my story has helped me tremendously and God has done a work in my heart shifting my perspective towards my healing process. I am so excited to rebuild our relationship, to talk about the things that have always been painful to discuss and to feel your warm embrace. I want to talk about the things that scare you, and things that may be painful. I would love to know more about your upbringing and how it shaped you into the man you are today. Although I am a woman now, there's a little girl inside of me that still yearns for your embrace. For so many years, I have searched for a man to fill your shoes and do the things you did effortlessly and where you missed. I set unrealistic goals for every man I *have encountered because they could never be you. You are my father and that's something another man can never be. I love you for who you were then, who you are now, and most importantly, who you will grow to be. God's mercy and grace is abundant, and I am happy that I can share my heart with you now. I love you Daddy, and I forgive you.*

    Signed,
    Daddy's Little Girl

Alicia R. Stokes & Tyeisha L. Dalton

Harvest

It's often said that what goes around comes back around. Even in scripture, God tells us, "Be not deceived; God is not mocked: for whatsoever a man soweth that shall he also reap." —Galatians 6:7 NIV. We often plant seeds out of brokenness and subject ourselves to rotten fruit and unpleasant harvests. We never fully understand the magnitude of our poor cultivation until we are out of a storm, yet weeds are still in the middle of our beautiful garden. My use of gardening and cultivation is quite ironic when it comes to describing the impact my mother had on my life. She's a natural at gardening; what one would consider as having a green thumb, I've watched her in complete awe soiling her land and producing and bearing one of God's most beautiful creations. A garden full of life, vibrant colors and tranquility.

If I could describe my mother in one word, "selfless" would be the perfect adjective. I watched her sacrifice her life, happiness, and peace at the expense of others. I know we are not to question the motive of our parents, but I often wonder how one person could give so freely of themselves. I recall having a unique relationship with my mom, as she spent a lot of time teaching me my school lessons, taking me on shopping trips and salon visits. She would reward me for doing my chores and getting good grades and I looked forward to the time we spent together. She showered me with gifts and materials but that could never measure up to what I really needed from her. I didn't need a friend or a shopping partner but a model of unconditional love. I understand now a person can only love in the way they know how, yet it doesn't take away the sting my young heart experienced.

GRACEFULLY BROKEN: A JOURNEY OF SELF-DISCOVERY

For much of my childhood even after my uncle's death, I suffered tremendously. I used to literally beat myself up about why I couldn't just tell my mom about the hell I was encountering. We had way too many girl days filled with shopping and pampering trips, so why couldn't I just rest my head on her lap and tell her about his sin? The truth is we never had a relationship where I felt comfortable enough to be vulnerable, to be transparent, to simply be me. I remember the days of wanting to tell my truth only to be met with frustration and impatience. I learned to deem my wound unimportant and master the art of wishful sublime. I prayed one day she'd see me.

My mom not "seeing me" caused me great pain. Those feelings of unworthiness and disgust intensified every passing year. Usually when children are exposed to traumatic things they tend to act out in school or within their social settings. My grades always flourished, and I never had an issue making friends, I simply internalized everything. I was conflicted with telling her my truth but carried anger she never asked. She was too busy with work, keeping my brother and I in private school and trying to keep my grandmother happy that she missed out on us, her family. She missed the nights I cried myself to sleep, or the countless bathroom trips I spent staring in the mirror utterly disgusted with the little girl looking back at me.

Unresolved issues and sins of the past always have a way of repeating in the present. I often wonder what other secrets have been swept under the rug in an attempt to protect family dynamics. I wanted so badly for my mother to just see the wounded little girl living inside her home, but she was too busy shielding and covering up her own wounds she couldn't possibly have seen mine. The relationship between my grandmother and mom was odd; there seemed to be a disconnect between the two. I didn't understand the bitterness or anger my mom carried for my grandmother until she mouthed four simple words to her in a heated argument: "You didn't see me." After hearing those words, emotions came rushing out of me like a lightning bolt. I remember running to the bathroom and simply breaking down. I said to myself repeatedly, "You didn't see me." What did she mean? I wanted so badly to ask her but as usual I suppressed my emotions because dealing with "why she didn't see me" was too painful...even for her. My mother and I are alike in many

ways. We search for approval and validation from others while missing the important things, the things of the essence.

Mark 5:34 Jesus said to the woman, "Daughter, your faith has healed you. Go in peace and be freed from your suffering." NIV

Dear Mommy

Mommy, I forgive you, I love you and you are truly my best friend. As a mother now, I realize just how much we are truly alike. I've waited so long to have the relationship we have now. I can come to you in my most vulnerable moments and just lay my head on your lap and cry out to you. I never had that before and now I understand more than ever the saying God makes everything new, and all things work together for the good. Growing up, I needed you to see me, needed you to embrace me but you cannot give what you don't have yourself. I understand that now. The little girl in me wanted a mother who would speak to the insecurities his sin had caused without the utterance of words, but you had your own insecurities you were facing. During my weakest moments, God had manifested in an intentional way his grace, favor and true understanding of a relationship between a mother and daughter was formed. The best love you have ever given me is showing me the love of God and His love outweighs anything I thought I needed back then or anything I could ever get from this world. Had we known that years ago, I am sure it would have prevented so much heartbreak, but I am thankful for where we are now. I am extremely grateful you never advised me to conform and do as the world says to do. You pray with me and always ensure that I do what God says to do, even when it hurts, and I don't want to. People tend to think following God is easy, but that's the furthest thing from the truth. Yet, watching you live your life for Him has opened my eyes to God's grace. I admire the way you handle my children; the patience you have with them, the way you see beyond the moment and can decipher what needs to be seen in the long run. I will no longer allow Satan to lie to me nor separate the bond we are forging. At one point, I used to watch with envy the way you love and pour into my children but now I am thankful generational curses are being broken and we can both give them the best parts of ourselves. Our last lucid conversation concluded with you asking me to forgive myself and move forward. teach my children the meaning of love as well as how to love, and God's word and to know I am, and will always be, more than enough. The sentiment and words shared touched my heart in ways I will never

Alicia R. Stokes & Tyeisha L. Dalton

have the ability to explain with words. I know God is intentional and everything you and I endured is working together for our good.

Mommy, I forgive you for not seeing me when I was a little girl but I'm thankful you see me now; I'm thankful we can spend hours talking about the painful stuff, things that leave us teary-eyed but then always ends in prayer, trusting, knowing and believing God has us covered. I love you, Mommy, and I am so thankful for the relationship we have now. You are truly my best friend.

Love you Always,

Alicia S

Chapter Two

Seed: Codependency

THE SEEDS OUR PARENTS' plant will always harvest in due time. My upbringing and his sin taught me early on to sacrifice my own personal needs to meet the needs of others. Unfortunately, it has been accompanied by passivity and feelings of shame, low self-worth, and insecurity. Ironically, I was always willing to save and "fix" someone else, but I was in the greatest need of fixing. I've come to learn I have this healing spirit that attracts broken people. Instead of me seeing the broken glass and shattered pieces for what they really are, somehow, I challenge myself to fix what's broken with them. The problem in and of itself is when you're just as broken as the person you are trying to "heal," then the broken pieces get entangled and feelings of guilt and responsibility for the suffering of others outweigh your own need for self-love and happiness.

I am a master at people-pleasing and my need for validation and approval has always been greater than my need for my own happiness. When I became of dating age, I always had a boyfriend and every one of them was a "project" to me. My first serious relationship was my sophomore year of high school. It started off as a friendship. Early on he became my best friend. He was someone I could talk to about any and everything. I remember rushing home from school, finishing homework and chores just to talk with him on the phone all night. Our relationship was like one I had never experienced before. I finally had someone who saw me. He made me feel good, he validated me, and he put me before anything. Looking

Alicia R. Stokes & Tyeisha L. Dalton

back, I can't quite understand how kids could have the love we had for one another. Outside of school and work, I spent every moment with him. I neglected my family, my friends—hell, everyone! He had become my addiction. My childhood abuse, combined with my silence, allowed me to enter a relationship that would soon become another poison.

For the first time in a long time, I felt good; I could be myself with him. He was my kryptonite. I didn't have to keep up with the façade or pretend to be anyone other than myself. I longed for someone to see me, and he did, and I was willing to protect that at all costs, even if it meant losing myself in the process. Our relationship progressed fast. I found myself barely out of high school, pregnant, and he was incarcerated. I remember crying to him on a collect call about what was next for us. Although I had just turned eighteen, I wanted my child, but I knew that he wanted more for me. He always had my best interest at heart, so collectively, we decided to terminate the pregnancy, allowing me to follow my dreams and go to college. I didn't tell my parents about it, as they'd surely be disappointed, so I did what I knew best, I hid it. I pushed myself through my morning sickness and attended my prom, high school graduation, all while pregnant and brokenhearted. This was just another one of those times where I felt the need to protect the people I love, even if it meant disregarding my feelings and ending an innocent life deserving to live.

I vividly remember not being able to sleep the night before my appointment. I wanted so badly for him just to call me and tell me that he changed his mind and that we would be alright, but he didn't. I thought my mom would catch on with my frequent trips to the bathroom. I wonder what it would have been like had she seen me. I just needed one person whom I loved to tell me it was okay, and I didn't have to go through with it. Unfortunately, that never happened. I went with a friend that very next day to get my abortion. Recalling the moment is such a blur. I just remember an extreme chill and intense pain. At that moment, I felt ashamed and guilty. I felt no different than the monster that stole my innocence. I didn't ask to be violated, and my child didn't ask to exist, and here I was, taking the innocent life I created.

It's almost like déjà vu. From that day forward, our relationship shifted, much like the relationship between my father and I. At the time, I didn't understand the breakdown in our relationship but looking back now it makes perfect sense. He was released from jail, and I was in my first year of college. I ended up going to a local university because he felt it was best for us to continue our relationship with me near, so of course, I stayed. I began to spend a lot of time at school and with friends trying desperately to focus on my studies. My parents were paying out-of-pocket for me to attend, and I didn't want to disappoint them by failing my classes. Not long after his release, I noticed a change in his behavior. He became controlling and very paranoid. He was always overprotective of me; initially, I thought it was cute to have a boyfriend that cared as much as he did. However, things began to make a change for the worst.

Wounded

Only a lover could wound so deep. Despite knowing everything I went through, he broke me and watched me bleed. I was wounded by the very hand that once held me close and protected me from a world that I was not prepared to face. For the life of me, I don't understand why I just didn't leave the first time. My belief and truth are subconsciously I needed him. By now, I allowed myself to become isolated from all my close friends. He and I lived on the same street, and I found myself staying more at his house than at my own. To a degree, I loathed being home with my parents and adopted the belief he wasn't intentionally trying to inflict pain on me. So, I stayed... And I begged him to change. There were many nights where we would cry together after he abused me. Looking into his eyes, I knew he wanted to change as badly as I needed him to;

but unfortunately, my need and his want wasn't quite good enough.

As the years progressed, it had gotten so bad, and I no longer knew who I was. We were together for three years, and I couldn't understand how the only person who saw me could hurt me the way he did. The breakup-to-makeup cycle went on for years. He would apologize for the abuse, and I made myself look past it because he needed me. Broken people always tend to be selfless givers since it shifts the focus from our own voids while pacifying our desire to feel needed. When he loved me, he filled every single void that I so desperately needed growing up. I was nothing but the same little girl who was traumatized and abused at the hands of someone who was supposed to love and look after me. Damn those cycles.

I wish I had walked away for good before the spring of 2005. Maybe had I been strong enough to stop the damn cycle, then his mom would still be alive. I'm still dealing with forgiving myself for this. I remember that night so vividly. We were arguing, and I wanted to go home and get ready for work. As I was walking through the living room to leave, he grabbed me by my hair and drug me back into his room. His mom heard the commotion and quickly came to my aid to try and break us up. Eventually, he let me go, and I went my separate way. I told myself that this was it; I was done. I cried the entire way to work, and I'd had enough. I sat in the parking lot, begging God to help me let him go. I knew no matter what I did, and he would never change. I was so focused on my moment with God I didn't even notice the stranger knocking on my window. I rolled the window down with tears in my eyes, and this lady whom I had never met said three simple words: let it go. This angel sent from above prayed with me and held me in her arms, and to this day, I could never forget her embrace. It was what I needed for so long, just someone to embrace me and tell me it would be okay. Looking back, I know for a fact God sent her to me. I only wish she was there when I learned of the awful news a few hours later.

I went to work and fought through the tears and the urge to answer his repeated calls. Eventually, the phone calls ended, and I continued with my day until I got a call from my older brother. He sounded frantic and told me I needed to come home. I asked him what was wrong, but he wouldn't tell me. After begging him to tell me what happened, he delivered the news that my boyfriend's mom had passed away from a heart attack. At that moment, my heart stopped. My knees buckled, and I fell to the floor, hoping this was all some misunderstanding, a nightmare, a silly prank—anything but the truth. I laid in the middle of the break room floor, frozen. I was sure that was the reason he was blowing me up, and I felt so guilty. How could I not be there for him when he needed me? I immediately called him back, and he answered and told me he was so sorry and that he didn't want to lose me. I wasn't expecting to talk about us or our toxic relationship.

After hearing him beg and plead as he always did, it dawned on me that he hadn't learned the news about his mom. I froze up, how could I be the one to tell him this? I didn't understand how I knew before him. Eventually, through tear-filled words, I gained the courage to tell him the news. He told me that he had just spoken with the family, and she was okay. I gained hope in thinking that maybe my brother had it all wrong. Three minutes later, he called me back, crying and screaming, confirming the news that I delivered was true. I was sure that God couldn't possibly want me to leave him, so I rushed home to be by his side.

To justify my need for love and validation, I made myself believe that it was "God's Plan," and despite everything I went through with this man, I couldn't leave him. Our relationship thrived off brokenness, fear of loneliness, and desperate need for validation. Over the course of several months, I suffered as the abuse became worse, which could have cost me my life. Making the decision to leave or stay were both very painful; he needed me. He had just lost his mother and had a little sister to take care of. I felt guilty, saddened, and angry that I was even considering walking away. Choosing to leave him was one of the hardest choices I have ever had to make.

Mark 11:25, "And when you stand praying, if you hold anything against anyone, forgive them, so that your Father in heaven may forgive you your sins." NIV

I Forgive You

    I forgive you for hurting me when I trusted you with the treasures of my heart. I was naked with you. It was something about our connection that allowed me to be vulnerable and truly be myself with you. Before we were lovers, we were best friends; you touched the most intimate parts of me without even touching me. The way you bragged and boasted about me was something every girl wants. You adored the ground I walked on, but that came with a cost. Until recently, I never understood how you could hurt me in the way that you did. I allowed myself to be naked with you. I shared every part of my soul with you, and your insecurities blinded you from my genuineness, causing you to inflict a pain that will be a part of me until the day I die. Truth be told, the pain you caused has shaped my perception of my relationships after you. I wanted to be anything other than myself because being myself would inevitably end in devastation. Every time you hit me, I made myself believe I deserved it, and if I worked hard enough, you would eventually see my worth. Now that I am on my journey to healing, I find myself praying for you, praying God heals your brokenness. I no longer hold anger or resentment in my heart towards you, and I no longer feel the need to run away from you or my past with you. I will face you, and I can say wholeheartedly that I forgive you. I've come to learn our relationship was needed to mold both of us. I truly forgive you and wish you nothing but peace, happiness, and joy.

    Truly,

Alicia S.

Chapter Three

Superman

LATE SUMMER OF 2005, I finally found the courage to leave him. Looking back, I'm not sure what the final straw was. All I knew was I'd had enough. Those few months of solitude were the loneliest. Being alone was foreign and painful to me. I had no one to take the attention off my brokenness. I had no one to try and "fix;" no one to validate the insecurities lying dormant within. I played with the idea of going back to my ex, even entertained it at times, because having someone claim to love me was better than being alone. At least, until I met him.

It was so unexpected. Our meeting was divine, I am sure of it. The night we met I was open, I was vulnerable, yet so guarded. I promised myself I would never allow another man to break my heart. It was something about him, though. I had to explore it. We exchanged numbers and the very next day I received a call from him. I was on my way to drop my cousin off to college and I had to pass through his city, so we made plans to see one another. From that day forward, frequent trips to his city were made. Every weekend turned into every evening fast. Looking back, it's clear he needed me as much as I needed him. I liked him so much and I knew if I exposed my true authentic self to him it would end in disaster. It was quite natural for me to put on a façade. I desperately needed him to like me as much as I liked him; I couldn't mess it up with my truth. I pretended to be everything I was not, and we fell for each other fast.

Things progressed rather quickly and before I knew it, I was pregnant yet again by a man I barely even knew. I remember telling him of the news and being terrified of his response. Surprisingly, he was very supportive and even suggested we keep the baby. I remember talking with him the night I delivered the news discussing baby names and what life would look like for us should we go through with it. It's absurd to think we were discussing baby names before discussing future goals and marriage. I honestly was unsure of what decision to make but I knew I didn't want to feel the way I felt before.

I ended up telling my parents about the pregnancy and it baffles me trying to even remember how I did it. From the moment I told them of my mishap, I felt extreme disappointment in myself. How could I let this happen again? My parents were supportive but disappointed in me as well. The hurt was evident, visibly on my dad's face and all I wanted to do was erase it. At that exact moment, I decided I could not keep this child. I told them that I wanted to get an abortion and called Superman and told him of my decision. I think he was saddened by my decision but supported my wishes. A week or so later, I went through with it but this time I was numb to it. I didn't want to feel, I didn't want to think about it, I didn't want to see the look of disappointment on my dad's face ever again. I've discussed this with Superman on a couple of occasions but never felt remorseful or even saddened by this until today.

The truth is I loved Superman so much, but I never allowed myself to feel nor receive his love. I was guarded, extremely broken and expected disappointment. I made myself believe that eventually he would hurt me. Looking back, I simply did not know how to love. *Wow!* I didn't see a model of marriage in my upbringing where love was expressed. My parents were married but their marriage looked nothing like the fairytales I read about. I didn't have a relationship with my parents where I could be transparent, be myself or even receive their love. I was too busy trying to protect them from my truth; I couldn't possibly receive the love they tried to give me. This is such a painful revelation to experience especially considering where Superman and I are now in our relationship. I must take full accountability in the fact that I am just as responsible for the breakdown in our marriage as he is. That stings!

You might ask why I call my husband "Superman." The truth is subconsciously he saved me. He saved me from having to face my truth and from going back to a very toxic relationship. My need for a man was imperative and he filled that need rather quickly. However, he was not a man, just a boy, and I was just a broken girl who entered the relationship expecting to receive my happiness from him. I am almost certain he expected the same from me. Our intentions and love have always been pure, as we were only loving each other in the manner in which we were taught. The daunting thing about this is we both have hurt each other in unimaginable ways seeking happiness in things outside of God. Things quickly spiraled out of control, only this time we brought two children in this world who would, unfortunately, inherit the consequences of our poor decisions. Our love for them and our need for each other caused us to wed and stay in a relationship built off insecurity, void, and loneliness. *Wow!* Another hard pill to swallow.

Admitting the truth is painful. Outside of molestation and toxic relationships, I didn't even know who I was. As I am writing, I am reflecting on all the times I told Superman I just wanted him to see his potential. The sad thing is I didn't even know my own. I was so focused on "making him better" and creating this damn fairytale that I lost sight of what mattered— I mattered, too. Growing up, my parents didn't see me. In my marriage, Superman didn't see me. But, hell, how could I fault them when I didn't even see me? Healing has revealed to me the saying, "hurt people, hurt people," is true.

Winter Wonderland

I was so caught up on what my life should look like after molestation and abuse that I kind of willed things into existence. On the outside looking in, Superman and I had it all. I was so focused on building this fairytale with him that I ignored warning signs God had given me before we wed. A week before my wedding, I found out that my husband-to-be was on a dating site claiming to be single and looking to have a good time. None of this was foreign to me though, there were always other women and always a mirror for me to stare into before bed each night, wondering why I wasn't good enough for him. My gut told me to call the wedding off but the life I had envisioned for us would not allow me to. I made myself believe one day he would see me, and I would be enough. That day has yet to come. I couldn't bear to disappoint my parents after they had spent thousands on my dream wedding. So, I married him on January 19, 2013.

I remember prepping for the day, getting dolled up, ready to stand before family and friends and profess my love and commitment to Superman. I recall getting ready to walk down the aisle and immediately getting sick. I felt as if I was going to faint, but I deemed it nerves and decided I was going to marry that man waiting for me at the altar. I walked down the aisle with tear-filled eyes, and I was certain that neither one of us was equipped for what marriage to one another would be like. I've come to learn he thought marriage would change us as much as I did. Boy, did we have it all wrong.

I spent eight months preparing for my Winter Wonderland and no time preparing myself for marriage. I've come to learn that marriage requires God to be the foundation. It requires the knowledge of self, selflessness, compromise and the will to fight as equals on the same team. We were two broken and insecure people who didn't know God, didn't know ourselves and didn't know what the hell we really wanted. The painful part is we used one another to pacify the pain dwelling inside of us long before we met. Life happened, and the Band-Aid we used to suppress our pain wore off with each passing year in our marriage. I wanted God to fix us, I wanted Him to put us back together again, to heal the brokenness that laid dormant within us. I wanted Superman to see the broken pieces of himself. I was certain if he saw them and worked on them, then we would be fixed. We cannot heal what we won't reveal, so this cycle of unhappiness and brokenness has plagued our marriage for years. Satan has had his way and we have allowed him to cause division, infidelity and ultimately, hardened hearts.

Once I began to truly know God, I realized I was fighting against spirits and principalities, and not flesh. Satan had his way for far too long and I decided I would no longer allow him to have his way with my family. It was Superman's birthday and normally we spent all his birthdays together, but this year he did not spend it with me. I let Satan play with every single insecurity that laid dormant within. I remember lying in bed crying for hours wondering what happened to us and why wasn't I good enough. I wasn't eating. I had lost over twenty pounds in less than a month and my children were yearning for their mother, but I couldn't see past the idea my marriage was failing, that my Winter Wonderland was ending abruptly. In a small still voice, God whispered, "Give it to me." Writing has always been healing for me, so I decided to write my feelings with pen and pad while crying out to God. I had already vented to my mother, to my friends and quite honestly, I was done with that. This time I needed more. While they loved me, God loves me more, and His desire is to heal us making us complete again, so on this day I poured out my heart to God and I have never been the same.

Dear God,

I am unsure of my next move, not sure what to do. I am tired of doing it my way because I always make a big mess of things. God, I am so bitter and angry right now towards my husband and my children and it has nothing to do with them and everything to do with me. God, I am asking you to heal the parts of me that are broken, continue taking the blinders off my eyes and unplugging my ears. In a world full of hate and evil, Lord, teach me to be more like your son. Teach me how to love my husband genuinely again. I have been so caught up on how I think it should be that I'm literally fighting to be divorced. I am not sure what's next, Lord. I do want my marriage, but I don't want it more than I want Your will for my life. Please teach me how to trust you. Lord, I am asking for your forgiveness. Please soften our hearts toward one another again. I must seek you in this, Jesus, please bring my husband closer to you, Lord. Do what You need to do so that he can hear Your voice and understand the magnitude of Your love, way deeper than the love I'll ever be able to give him. Lord, protect him, keep him and watch over him. Teach me how to let him go and give complete reign to you. God, I am letting this marriage go and giving it to You today. I want Your will to be done even if it means I must walk away from all of this. I pray this in Your son, Jesus' name. Amen

Alicia R. Stokes & Tyeisha L. Dalton

Finally, that very day, I had given God complete control over my marriage. With each passing day, my perspective changed. I lost myself in our marriage and when things didn't go as I had envisioned, I didn't think life was worth living. I had finally learned to give up this fairytale I had planned for us and learned to just see things for what they were. Two broken people trying to love one another when we didn't even love ourselves. I asked myself countless times how a "good" God could possibly want me in a "bad marriage." How could he want me to suffer, why couldn't I just be happy? Why couldn't he just change? The more I questioned God about these very things, the more he showed me myself. I was faced with conviction. It's extremely difficult to look inward and identify the ways in which I contributed to the troubled pastures in my marriage. I began to understand how God could be using my marriage to bring me to a deeper faith and repentance. Using my marriage to remind me of the covenant I made with God and God alone. Right now, I am uncertain what the future holds; however, I do know that I've been fighting the wrong enemy for so many years. While in this storm, I'll continue to focus on his truth and not my feelings because Satan has been feeding me everything I "feel like" for years.

1 Corinthians 13:4-7

"Love suffers long and is kind; love does not envy; love does not parade itself, is not puffed up, does not behave rudely, does not seek its own, is not provoked, thinks no evil, does not rejoice in iniquity but rejoices in the truth; bears all things, believes all things, hopes all things, endures all things." NKJV

Husband,

I first want to acknowledge and thank you for all you have done for your family. When we met, we were both kids and didn't know a thing about love, yet we were inseparable. I watched you grow from a boy into a young man, conquering and overcoming some pretty hard challenges. You have taught me about strength and determination. It was you who went from flipping burgers to make ends meet, to relocating to another state without a place to lay your head for the betterment of your family. I could never thank you enough for that sacrifice. I also want to apologize for giving you such a hefty role to fill…SUPERMAN. How could I put such a heavy burden on you, you're only human learning your way as I am. On this journey, we have hurt each other tremendously and outside of all the pain I've endured I realized I loved you more than I loved myself, and that's where I was wrong. I'm on a journey toward healing and I want nothing more than for you to experience God's peace as I have, but you're not ready and finally, I am okay with that. I played God for so long and at this very moment I give that up. I am not Him and I have no control for His will for our lives. I want to forgive you first for the burden you placed on me, the burden to make you happy. You see, I now understand happiness is more of an inside job than an outside one and it's your responsibility to make you happy, not mine. I spent so many nights wondering why I was not good enough, why I couldn't make you happy, but the truth of the matter is; that was never my job. I forgive you for all the other women you entertained for the satisfaction of your ego. I forgive you for using me as your emotional punching bag. Those wounds were the hardest to get over; physical scars heal way faster than emotional ones, yet I still forgive you. I forgive you for not honoring and valuing me as your wife. Most importantly, I forgive you for hurting me. I understand more than ever that hurt people hurt people. I understand it was never your intention to purposely hurt me and because of that, I can see you as a young man learning your way and growing into the man you are destined to be. I told you when we wed that I love you and I always will. I love you enough to release you because I now understand your happiness is bigger than the voids you use to fill. Forgiving you when I hadn't received an apology, was extremely difficult for me. For so many years, I've done everything in hopes you would choose me and as bad as facing reality hurts, this time you don't

Alicia R. Stokes & Tyeisha L. Dalton

have to make that choice because I choose me. Life with you has taught me; love is a choice and you wake up daily choosing to be committed to your life partner. Love is way more of a choice than feelings...feelings fade. My hope is that one day you understand this. I pray for you daily and I will continue to pray not only for you but also for your soul. I pray that you understand that happiness, true happiness, can only be found in God and within yourself. People will always fail you. Please forgive me for making you pay and suffer for what my uncle did to me. Forgive me for turning into the controlling abuser I once despised. Looking back, I realize how manipulative and controlling it is to try to change you into the person I thought you should be. Forgive me for not giving you to God a long time ago. Had I focused on His truth and not my feelings, things may have been different between us. Forgive me for not knowing how to be submissive or yielding to you. My words have been emasculating and uncompromising and I haven't always given my best as your wife. Nonetheless, I love you and I'm excited that I can finally write about our part, the good, the bad and the ugly. I'm thankful for it all and I would never change meeting you. You and I were destined to meet and I'm thankful for all the good times we shared and even the bad ones because they propelled purpose. I pray one day you're able to heal from everything you went through even the hurt I caused you. Please understand it was never intentional. I'm most thankful that you played an integral part in molding and shaping me into the woman I am today. I love you and I forgive you.

Love Always

Chapter Four

Good Intentions

I WAS ONLY TWENTY-TWO when I bore my first child. I didn't have a clue about parenting or all the obstacles I would face raising a black son. The truth is subconsciously I was just a little girl who thought having a child would fix the broken pieces of my life. I never knew what unconditional love felt like until I had my son, Isaac. I was never open or even receptive to it until I laid eyes on him. For once, my life had meaning, and I promised myself that I would be a better woman for him. However, promises without God being the foundation is a recipe for disaster. As bad as it hurts to admit this, for quite some time I had been very toxic to my son. A hurt and damaged mother will repeat what's not repaired. I suppressed the trauma I encountered for well over twenty years and, unfortunately, innocent people ended up paying for sins they didn't commit, including my child. Although my intentions have always been pure, and my love has been genuine, you can't give what you don't have. For many years, I didn't see my son. I stayed busy in an attempt to protect my child from my brokenness. I missed out on so much of his life chasing a degree, more money, and convincing myself I was doing it for him. The truth is I was attempting to fill a void that can only be filled by God. I understand this to be true because I gained all those things and was still broken.

Alicia R. Stokes & Tyeisha L. Dalton

Isaac,

Mommy loves you so very much. I am so well-pleased with the young man you are growing into. From the day I laid eyes on you, I knew you would be amazing. You might not understand what I am about to do right now but one day you will, and my only hope is that you will forgive me for the pain I caused you. I was emotionally abusive, using you as a container for my rage, the rage my uncle caused me. You are not responsible for my brokenness and emptiness. Right now, Mommy is working hard on her healing and it's very important that you understand that I never meant to intentionally hurt you. My hopes for you are grand. I hope you are able to forgive me and continue to grow into the young man God has called you to be. I never want you to lose sight of who you are. Mommy tells you all the time that hurt people, hurt people and we must go to God for our happiness. I want you to know that there is a King in you and there is nothing in this world you cannot accomplish. I have had it wrong for so long but now I get it; the best love that I can give you is God's word. You are an amazing little boy and I know you have the potential to do anything you want. I've seen it. I've seen you be so down on yourself believing you weren't good enough. As I look back, you only mirrored what your mommy felt while you were in my womb. Son, you are more than enough, and I hope you know that. I love you, and no matter what, I will always keep you lifted in prayer.

Love Mommy

Three months after my husband and I wed, along came my pregnancy with Ivy. I had been convinced this pregnancy would be us having a girl and all my hopes were coming true. Ivy is more than what I imagined her to be. She is so full of charisma and sass with the right amount of compassion. They say your second child is a little easier. I find that to be the furthest thing from the truth. Both of my children are different, and they require different versions of me. While Isaac taught me, unconditional love, Ivy taught me accountability. Looking at her is like looking in the mirror and staring into the eyes of the innocent little girl I lost so long ago. The little girl who once was so full of life and allure. There is nothing more heart-rending than knowing that life can possibly do to her what I allowed it to do to me if I fail to stop Satan in his tracks. For generations, the women in my family have sought out approval and validation from others all while compromising their truest authentic selves. I've decided, the enemy's time is up, and it ends with me. I am holding myself accountable for teaching her how to maneuver through life without losing her elegance and God-given grace.

Alicia R. Stokes & Tyeisha L. Dalton

Ivy,

Princess, you light up my entire life. From the moment you were conceived, I knew you were going to be my angel. God knew I would need a replica of myself. I looked in your eyes, I was able to capture your innocence and it reminded me of what I had lost so long ago. Watching you grow up to be the young lady God has called you to be, has been nothing short of amazing. You are so kind-hearted; you wear your heart on your sleeves and you care about everyone you encounter. My only hope is that the pouring of your love comes from overflow and not depletion. It's imperative you know your value and your worth because if you don't then you'll allow other people to assign it to you. I will tell you until the day I die that you are more than enough, you are who God says you are. Our moments together, both good and bad, have allowed me to share things I wish my mother would have shared with me. I am making it a point to end the generational curse over the women in our family. The need for approval and validation has always prevailed over our own happiness. Your happiness matters, Ivy. God called you to live a meaningful life, one filled with joy and so much love that even when storms arrive, you're able to rest in God's peace knowing everything you endure will work together for your good. Please don't allow this world to diminish that sparkle in your eyes. When life seems overwhelming and your back is against the wall, remember the prayers that you and I share together. Remember God thinks you are wonderfully made, that you deserve the best. Ivy, there's no better truth than God's truth. I love you so much and I am so thankful that God blessed me with such a sassy little angel. You are, and always will be, MORE THAN ENOUGH!

Love, Mommy

Proverbs 22:6

"Train up a child in the way he should go; even when he is old, he will not depart from it." KJV

Chapter Five

Triggers-50 Shades of Brown

"Mommy, what's black? That little girl over there told me I can't play with her because I'm black," said my inquisitive brown little boy at the tender age of three. He had tears streaming down his face. At that moment, everything I hated about myself had swelled up in the form of anger and rage as I tried to make sense of what was happening and why I couldn't control nor justify my emotions. I learned to suppress my blackness so to speak, but standing in the face of a child, my child, having to explain to him why he was hated based on the color of his skin cut me deep. In fact, it opened, yet another wound I was not ready to face. How could I teach my son to love himself when I hated the very blackness that clothed my shattered wounds?

Growing up, my parents sacrificed a lot. Not only did they sacrifice their peace, healing, and sanity but they also ensured they exposed my brother and I to a world that looked nothing like our home front. I went to predominantly white schools from grade school through high school and never had a problem adjusting to my environment. As I mentioned earlier, hiding behind a facade had become an art for me, so fitting in was never a real issue until I, like my son, was reminded of my blackness. I hung out with a group of white girls all throughout middle school. They were the in-crowd, popular, privileged and in my eyes the most beautiful girls I had ever seen. There I was, a black girl, plagued with not only sexual abuse but self-hate because not only was I black, I was dark-skinned. My school best-friend, Olivia, was having a graduation party and it was the talk of the town. I felt honored to be her friend and was excited and anxious to attend. The anxiety was met with sheer heartbreaking disappointment the night before her party as she disclosed her dad felt it was in the best interest for me not to attend, as the neighbors wouldn't understand. I was forced to live with my shattered blackness in a predominantly white school with faces that looked nothing like mine. I thought that if I mirrored their existence, talked and walked like them, styled my hair like them, they would accept and approve of me. Olivia's dad showed me that no matter how hard I tried to "fit in," I was in fact still black!

In my neighborhood, I could be "myself." I could be in tune with my blackness; however, I was too black for the likings of some of my peers. I remember being taunted and teased about the color of my skin. I truly hated my existence. Many nights, I would cry to my mom about how I was treated, begging her to find a product that could lighten my blackness and make me prettier. Any male attention I got was unwarranted. I couldn't believe that someone would want me. I was quickly reminded, however, that I was "pretty to be dark-skinned" or that they didn't usually talk to dark-skinned girls but would make an exception for me. Those very cruel and insensitive words still haunt me to this day. I came to believe that I was just an ugly black girl with wounds. So, watching my son cry about why he wasn't "good enough" to play on the slide with a girl of a different race hurt me in a way I'll never be able to explain with mere words alone. At that time, I was still dealing with self-love issues, so I didn't know how to console him or speak to the king in him. I was angry, I was hurt, and I felt like a helpless little girl all over again.

I spent many days staring at my reflection, attempting to find some way to love the little girl staring back at me. I was always sought after and reminded of my beauty, but I didn't believe it to be so. Someone else telling me only satisfied my need for validation now. My issues with the shade of my skin did not subside until I enrolled in an Africana studies class in college. My history lessons up until that point were whitewashed and subjective. It took a professor to passionately teach about my blackness and the blackness of my ancestors to allow me to open up to accepting myself and being proud of the skin I was in. I slowly came around to merely "liking" my reflection.

Beautiful Brown Girl

Dear Brown Girl,

You are more than enough! You are beautiful. The sun radiates off the melanin that clothes your inner beauty. I know the cruel remarks may have tainted your self-esteem, the watered-down "compliments" may have made you feel less than, the reflection looking back at you may have been plagued with self-hate; however, I am here to change the narrative. You are a Goddess draped in God's finest creation: melanin. This letter was written to remind you of how powerful and resilient you truly are. As a young woman, it was extremely hard not to internalize the message that dark skin is forbidden, second class and not pretty. Growing up, the women in the magazines and plastered all over TV were of a lighter complexion and most of my male counterparts didn't think twice about voicing their opinion and preference. When I was reminded of my beauty, I didn't believe it, I didn't see it. Even now, I still struggle at times with insecurities systematically imposed on us during slavery. Systems that encouraged and propelled division and colorism among our race, which have trickled down generations. We are at war with one another. We have been taught to compete and work against one another, not truly understanding sisterhood, no matter the shade of our skin, is such a tremendous force! The lie that I am unpretty and not good enough always comes back, but now I know who I am, I know what God says about me. If you still struggle with identity and self-love issues, I understand. I was there before. I encourage you to get in a mirror as much as possible and begin to love on yourself, every inch of you because you are in fact wonderfully and fearfully made. It took tremendous soul searching, even more sleepless nights, but now I can walk with my head held high because my melanated skin, my

Alicia R. Stokes & Tyeisha L. Dalton

kinky hair, my full lips and protruded nose don't define my beauty. I am who God says I am. I am in fact more than enough and you are, too, beautiful brown girl!

Love Alicia S

Psalm 139:13-16

For you formed my inward parts; you knitted me together in my mother's womb. I praise you, for I am fearfully and wonderfully made. Wonderful are your works; my soul knows it very well. My frame was not hidden from you, when I was being made in secret, intricately woven in the depths of the earth. Your eyes saw my unformed substance; in your book were written, every one of them, the days that were formed for me, when yet there was none of them. ESV

#MeTooMovement

There was a time when even the thought of sexual abuse made me cringe. Certain smells would trigger me and incidents involving children always made me uncomfortable. It seemed to always haunt me when I thought I had completely healed from the traumatic things I encountered. The truth of the matter is healing is an ongoing process and I will probably have these specific triggers for the rest of my life. I'm just thankful I have a release now. The Me-Too Movement has brought so much light to such a sensitive and controversial topic. Sometimes it serves itself as a temporary debriding agent, forcing a wound to reopen every time a new story of sexual abuse and molestation hits social media. Numerous men and women from all walks of life are opening and sharing their truths, and any feelings of guilt I encounter seem to always subside once they reveal their truths.

I know all too well what it's like to be a small child forced into womanhood by the hands of someone who was supposed to protect her. I would lay in bed and literally tremble as I heard him stumble into my grandmother's house drunken and abrupt. The alcohol on his breath still plagues me to this very day, yet ironically any sexual escapade I encounter is only as satisfying as my inebriated high. Along with my innocence, he also robbed me of my sexual appetite; being vulnerable sexually or even enjoying the act has been quite the task.

Absurdly enough, I fell in love and married a man whose appetite for sex is very heightened, to say the least. I've struggled with satisfying him and aiding my insecurities for well over ten years, and as odd as this sounds, I excused a lot of his behavior because of my inadequacy. Having someone long for me sexually always seems to intensify my insecurity with my body, my sexual appetite and my ability to please a man. While I try so hard to have grace for what my uncle has done to me, it's extremely difficult when I face moments like this. Moments where I am forced to recall all the nights, he would touch me in forbidden places, places I wished I could have shared with a man who valued me. Most importantly, places I wish I could have shared on my own terms.

Healing from sexual abuse is painful and I can only imagine all the stories that go untold. Each story withheld holds an immense pain that can only subside with release. I look back over my life and all the years I kept this painful secret to myself to save my loved ones, yet I caused myself such immeasurable pain. In 2015, the unaddressed pain led me to a hospital bed surrounded by psychiatrists and physicians trying to my sense of my suicide attempt. My husband and I had gotten into an argument, my son laid in his bed crying and I stood there next to my son's bed broken. I felt like a failure; at parenting, being a wife, hell just being a woman. I had been prescribed pain meds from a prior accident and decided to take my life. I locked myself in the bathroom and took a handful of them. You see, to the outside world I had it together but inside I was literally dying. I felt death had to be better than the hell I was living. As I lay in the hospital bed crying one phone call from my son put my life into perspective and I knew at that very moment that if I couldn't live for myself, I owed it to my children to live for them. It was there on that hospital bed I decided I would heal; I would tell my parents about the hell I suffered as a child. My parents called me several times trying to make sense of what happened with me. Finally, they saw me, so I shared the hell I had endured for well over 20 years. I finally told them about the sexual abuse. I told my mom about her brother and how he robbed me of my innocence. I cried out to my dad about the change in our relationship and how I felt unprotected. My healing began at that moment and to this day continues to exist. My mom and I talked for quite some time about the abuse and my feelings. After I acknowledged I had a problem with release and forgiveness my mom suggested I go to counseling. I have been in counseling for the last 4 years and it has helped me tremendously. I have been able to sort through my feelings, better my relationships and most importantly take back control of my life.

Alicia R. Stokes & Tyeisha L. Dalton

Tell Somebody

To Whom It May Concern,

The scrutiny that comes with victimization, whether it's sexual, physical or mental abuse, is quite painful to navigate through. You're often left wondering what you did to deserve the traumatic experiences you endured. I am here to tell you that no matter what the world says, it is not your fault. Unfortunately, we live in a broken world full of hurt and damaged people who hurt people to heal themselves. The world will tell you to pay evil with evil and to continue existing with bitterness and hatred in your heart. But just as that sounds, it's not the avenue to take towards healing. God is the way, the truth, and the light, and as I embark on the journey towards self-discovery and healing, I'm amazed at what He has done for me and through me. I want to tell you, you are not alone, and God has beauty for those ashes. When the time is right, I challenge you to tell your story no matter how painful. You owe it to yourself and to other people who are struggling with the very thing you're struggling with right now. I challenge you to seek God, to forgive yourself and, yes, to forgive your abuser(s). Although it can never erase the memories or the pain caused, there is freedom in forgiveness. I stand with you and I am your voice until you're able to speak your truth.

Love Alicia S

2 Corinthians 1:3-7

"Praise be to the God and Father of our Lord Jesus Christ, the father of compassion and the God of all comfort, who comforts us in all our troubles so that we can comfort those in any trouble with the comfort we ourselves receive from God. For just as we share abundantly in the sufferings of Christ, so also our comfort abounds through Christ. If we are distressed, it is for your comfort and salvation; if we are comforted, it is for your comfort, which produces in your patience, endurance of the same sufferings we suffer. And our hope for you is firm, because we know that just as you share in our sufferings, you also share in our comfort." NIV

The Chains are Breaking

It's incredibly difficult to write about a storm you're experiencing while you are in the middle of it. Ironically, I never thought I would experience peace while in it or even see the other side of it. As I reflect on everything I have been through, I am most thankful that the pain had a purpose. There were many nights I would cry, asking God, "Why Me?" But now I'm more concerned with what God is trying to show me. Now I understand more than ever each tear that falls is bursting with such powerful lessons. While I prepare myself for the next chapter in my life, I can't help but question the unknown. I have spent my entire life trying to control what happens, so the feeling of vulnerability has always been an issue for me. Today I am deciding this is where it ends. I've never had a problem forgiving others but for the life of me, I can't forgive myself or the man that made me a woman at such a young age. I now understand that is where the healing must begin.

Alicia R. Stokes & Tyeisha L. Dalton

Dear Uncle,

You hurt me when you were supposed to protect me. I've spent most of my adult life suppressing the pain you caused me. You violated me, you took my innocence away and you left me to wallow in it. I spent most of my life angry, unsure of myself and deeply pained. Somehow, through all of that, I thought I was big enough to solve not only my problem but everyone else's. I was determined to be a superhero to save people from feeling how I was feeling, and, in the end, it's all been detrimental for me. I've tried to buy people's love to show my worthiness because you made me feel like I was worthless. I was willing to do anything and to accept anything just for someone to see my worth. Why would you do that to a child? What happened to you to allow you to cause a child so much trauma? I've suffered for so long and today I am done. The cycle ends now. It's taking everything in me to really forgive you. I've played with this idea of forgiving you for years, but today… I forgive you.

Your niece, Alicia

2 Corinthians 2:5-17 ESV

"Now if anyone has caused pain, he has caused it not to me, but in some measure—not to put it too severely—to all of you. For such a one, this punishment by the majority is enough, so you should rather turn to forgive and comfort him, or he may be overwhelmed by excessive sorrow. So, I beg you to reaffirm your love for him. For therefore I wrote that I might test you and know whether you are obedient in everything. Anyone whom you forgive, I also forgive. Indeed, what I have forgiven, if I have forgiven anything, has been for your sake in the presence of Christ, so that we would not be outwitted by Satan; for we are not ignorant of his designs."

Alicia R. Stokes & Tyeisha L. Dalton

Dear Alicia,

We repeat what we don't repair. This wound you've been aiding is not your fault, but the healing is your responsibility. I know you have been hurt in unimaginable ways; I've felt your heartbreak repeatedly. I've tasted the tears as you've cried yourself to sleep not wanting to wake up to face another day. I've witnessed you hide behind the mask of a smile and put everyone else before you. I've been there with you every step of the way. We have cried both happy and painful tears and we have not been okay for a very long time. Some days, I spend hours looking at you in the mirror, trying to make sense of the woman you have become. You are so compassionate, so forgiving, undeniably strong, so resilient, yet at times I question that strength—the motive behind it. Are you still seeking validation and approval from others? Are you still taking on the burden of "fixing" others? Why are you still holding on? Where do you go from here? I'm sure truthfully answering these questions will be no easy task, yet your transparency has the power to set the scene for the next chapter in your life and for generations to come. I dare you to ask God what He is trying to show you as you navigate answering these questions, and when the time is right I ask that you are honest because this time you owe it to yourself!

In the meantime, I want you to forgive yourself for not speaking about his sin. It started when you were just seven years old. A little girl fascinated with barrettes, bows, princesses, dollhouses and barbie dolls, yet forced into womanhood before you had even the slightest inkling of who you were. I have been here with you all along, helping you to carry this burden and it has become too big for us to handle alone. Now it's time to put the bag down and use our voice to speak about his sin; but most importantly, forgive.

I want you to forgive yourself for committing to a relationship while stained with molestation, unworthiness and low self-esteem. I understand your need to fill those voids and I am ecstatic that you are in a place of self-reflection and accountability now. I want you to forgive yourself for thinking you had the power to change someone else while you struggled for well over twenty years trying to change yourself and address your own issues.

I love that you have come to a place of counteracting this whole "grass is greener on the other side" theory. You finally understand that you must take "you" on the "other side." Your dedication to your relationship with God, your mental health and your family is noteworthy.

I dare you to move forward in life fearlessly, unapologetically, but most importantly, with confidence. You've finally reached a point where you've closed chapters that once drained you. I commend you for speaking out about your past hurts and taking accountability for the mistakes you've made. I find it even more admirable that you choose to encourage and uplift others even while you are in a storm. The woman you have become is astounding. You have the power, the confidence and the will to not only end generational curses within your own family but in other families alike. Your willingness to share your story in a vulnerable and transparent way will plant the seeds for accountability, forgiveness and above all, love. You are leaving a legacy to your children and to this world. I love you!

Love You, Alicia

Hebrew 4:16 NIV

"Let us then approach God's throne of grace with confidence, so that we may receive mercy and find grace to help us in our time of need."

Alicia R. Stokes & Tyeisha L. Dalton

Broken Crayons Still Color

    As I reflect on everything I have been through, I am amazed that I am still standing and able to share my story with others. There were so many days I did not want to get off the floor. I begged God to end my life because I couldn't bear to face another day. Unforgiveness has caused me mental incarceration for much of my adult life. I've paid for crimes I didn't commit and hurt people along the way because I didn't understand the power and magnitude of forgiveness. I vow to never again be that woman who laughs or ridicules another woman's tears. I vow to never emasculate our men, our sons, our fathers. I won't be that woman who subconsciously passes on toxicity to her children. I never again want to be that woman who can't look in the mirror and face herself.

    This season I am currently in solidifies my pain having a purpose. Though I cannot see the other side I know what God has for me is better than anything I could've ever imagined for my life. My upbringing may have been filled with the devastating trauma of molestation, I have suffered great pain from past relationships, and my marriage isn't the fairytale I envisioned it to be, but I dare not let those feelings overwhelm the season that God has me in. God makes all things new when you trust and believe in Him and I know that He has my back, and this too shall pass.

    While it's extremely easy to blame others' inequities on the sins of our past and skeletons in our closets, life has taught me everyone is ultimately responsible for their own individual choices. Living a life that's anything less than abundant and fulfilling is the direct result of our own inability to embrace the gift of forgiveness and grace that Jesus so freely gave us. At the end of this life, the only person I will have to answer for is myself, not my parents, grandparents, uncles, aunts, spouse, children and grandchildren. In fact, my family tree stretches back much farther than I will ever be able to imagine. There is an "Eve" and "Adam" in all of us; my story solidifies that. Yet, even still, God's grace is sufficient, and His forgiveness is forever encompassing.

Ephesians 2:8-10 NIV

"For it is by grace you have been saved, through faith—and this is not from yourselves, it is the gift of God—not by works, so that no one can boast. For we are God's handiwork, created in Christ Jesus to do good works, which God prepared in advance for us to do."

Afterword

I REMEMBER THE DAY I met Alicia like it was yesterday. It was our first day at Lutheran High East, Old Testament class. Here I am, this quiet, shy, freshman in this new school filled with new faces. I was a bit of a "lame," so I grabbed the first seat in front of the class and sat patiently, awaiting the start of the lecture. Everyone else entered the classroom and got settled at their desks, including the teacher. As soon as Mr. Essenburg stood in front of the class for his introduction, Alicia blurted out an extremely corny joke about his appearance. The entire class paused, turned towards her with a look of confusion, I chuckled loudly, although it was so quiet you could hear crickets chirp.

"Hey, you! Girl in the front! Come sit back here, next to me," Alicia said as she rubbed the chair next to hers. Without hesitation, I moved my seat and introduced myself.

"Hey, I'm Dominique. What's your name?" I said.

"I'm Alicia. I have a feeling we're going to be the best of friends."

Almost twenty years later, and we are surely the best of friends.

Alicia is one of the most amazing women I know, and I am truly blessed and honored to have her in my life. Our friendship started from a humorous moment and we kept the same energy to this day. There is not a second that goes by where we are not laughing, and she is still cracking corny ass jokes! While we've also struggled, cried and hurt together, we have always been sure to uplift one another and find the beauty in any situation we face.

We've both been through so much and experienced great pain at a very young age. When she first told me about her experience with her uncle, my heart sank. I had no idea! I knew she'd been through some things—we all have, right? That's a part of life. I had no clue she'd endured such agony and I instantly hated him, just as much as she did. We hear about such horror far too often. So many people sustain abuse and have no effective *healing* from it, instead, they are just *dealing* with it. Alicia suffered for so long before finding God, herself and her voice. It wasn't until then that she gained the strength and courage to face her tribulations and begin healing. In doing so, she has blossomed into an even brighter, stunning woman with a powerful and inspiring testimony.

It is much easier to blame someone else for our pain and lack of happiness than it is to be accountable and take action. It is common for us to sweep certain behavior under the rug in hopes that it will go away or handle itself. Even if we say we will address it later, many of us do not, not realizing we have only made things far worse and much harder to heal from. We get so caught up in how we think people and life should be and have the nerve to be upset when things don't go according to our plan. But that's just it; our plan and God's plans are totally different!

This book has revealed the importance of self-reflection and accountability. More importantly, *Gracefully Broken* has shown me how knowing, trusting and loving God changes altogether narratives and perspectives. These women are not "bible thumpers" nor claim to be flawless, Jesus-like, perfect women who practice God's will "to a T." They are human, just like us. They are living and finding their way, just like us. Both have made mistakes and even steered away from God's path, just like us.

Three profound words to describe this book are: relatable, enlightening and uplifting. This read evoked diverse emotions, from sadness and guilt to joy and peace. If these women can walk in their shoes as graciously as they are, why

Alicia R. Stokes & Tyeisha L. Dalton

can't we do the same? It's time to break generational curses and set the stage for love, happiness, peace, and success. It's time we focus on our own imperfections rather than the next person's. Use these stories as motivation to face your problems and turn to God for guidance. For He is the key to all happiness!

Part 2

Acknowledgments

WRITING THIS BOOK HAS been such a great release, and I am privileged to share my life and story with you. I appreciate your support of our book. It is my prayer that you learn from my story and find the courage to overcome all that life throws your way. I was born into this world to fulfill a purpose. I still have not reached the fullest potential of that fact. I strive every day to be positive, loving, and driven to complete God's will in my life. I want to first give thanks to God for His protection over my life and the creative abilities I possess.

I would like to thank all the people in my life that have impacted me and pushed me to grow. To Sean Holland, my Pastor and spiritual advisor, thank you for teaching me the power God gifted me with…to be a mighty woman of God, pushing through adversity. To First Lady Tayana Holland, you are the epitome of womanhood and I appreciate your leadership. To Willie Dalton Sr. and Anna Dalton, my loving grandparents. You saved my life. Thank you for your love and dedication to your family. Papa, rest peacefully.

To my beautiful children: Iyana, Ian, and Peyton. My calm and chill side. My sweet, funny, sensitive-yet-tough side. And, my accountability. You are the greatest gifts God has given me. Always remember that.

S.I.P., my *Sisters In Power*. Especially my Aunt LaTonya Dalton, Cecelia Wilison, Shantae Johnson, Frances Howard, and Jasmine Booker. Lenee Mancina, Deandrea Vines, Charnise Floyd, Kimberly Norris, and many more. I want to thank you, ladies, for loving and pushing me to be the best version of me through your selflessness, attentiveness and cheering me on.

Elon Geffrard, Deja Williams, and Akia Joi: I appreciate your selfless pouring and spiritual covering. I have learned so much about grace, forgiveness, and love from you. Thank you! Terika Westbrook, my sister, Jhamal Swift, Shari Ivery, Pastor Howard, and First Lady Charlissa McWilliams, what can I say about the love you show my children as godparents? I am humbled and appreciative of your support and love.

To my mom, Christine Dalton I appreciate and love you. I have learned and loved through you and with you and I see the beauty in your journey. God is repairing the broken places and we are continually rebuilding. To those who have transitioned: Boise and Matilda Breakfield, David and Ernestine Buford, Ray Green, my father, and the many people in my village that took care of me and loved me as if I were their flesh and blood. Rest peacefully. I hope you are proud of me. I am forever grateful to each of you. I love you.

~ Tyeisha L. Dalton

Introduction

"German philosopher Walter Benjamin had the curious notion that we could change the past. For most of us, the past is fixed while the future is open". -Terry Eagleton

THERE IS A GREAT strength that a woman experiences in giving birth to a child. In birthing and raising three children, I realize that there is so much power and greatness developed in the womb. Before we were placed in our mother's care, God carved-out a life for us. Only He holds the key and the knowledge to our lives. We make plans and He laughs because He's already predestined us to live according to His will, not ours.

The plan I decided on was going to college, meeting Prince Charming, obtaining a wonderful, stable career and, ultimately, buying a house with the proverbial white picket fence. The natural progression of marriage and children would follow, of course. I would be a mother, I was certain of this. Especially as an only child, I wanted a large family.

The ideas in my mind were established, but my plan had a flaw because I failed to stay "in order." Many would say that I *put the cart before the horse*, so I believed that I had lost my way. This path, ultimately, lead me into motherhood before marriage as I was distracted by my mistakes. Mistakes are bound to happen; but you press through and, hopefully, you grow because of them. When overcoming the trials of life, it is the journey that produces greatness. And, it often deviates from your plans. For me, the pain was all I could see.

History shows us that some of the greatest inventors, scientists, thinkers, and leaders have had "bumps in the road" and they've succeeded. With that, I've had to remind myself that I will "make it" despite the path I envisioned for myself. It's just that I would require the longer route. As I was trying to gain control of my life, carefully placing my footing so that I could keep from falling, I continued to attack my dreams with vigor and passion along the way. Not losing sight or focus and aspiring to have -and be- more than before.

Each day God grants us a fresh anointing. The more I imagined where I wanted to be, the more my thoughts increased to where I had been. It can be very distracting and we often fail to get past what has been lost. Many battles have been won pushing through the storms that come and go. Many are fought alone and in silence, some loud and in public but the Lord is a present help through it all, for this I am certain. Without Him, I would have surely fallen, committed suicide, aborted dreams, given up. And the enemy would have won.

We are all born into this life with a passion and an innate desire to be great. The circumstances of our birth precedes the possibilities of the future. So we must consider the premature baby or the runt of the litter for just a moment. Statistically, the mortality rates are high. Both, Doctors and Veterinarians alike, will warn that the premature baby or runt of the litter could potentially face complications and, in some instances, even death. Here is where the tables can turn. The uncertainty of it all is obvious, but the percentage of those who beat the odds and survive…well, those numbers are equally staggering. A person's internal instinct or desire for surviving can change any circumstance. We are born to fight! The time is now to push through the current storm. The enemy knows when a person gets close, so he attacks the mind. He wants us to use our bodies, self-esteem, self-worth, and value to acquire the love Mom and Dad never gave.

Throughout my writing, I would often listen to songs on repeat. There were several that ministered to me. Jonathan McReynolds has a song called "Cycles" and part of the lyrics say that "the devil learns from your mistakes, even if you don't". This stuck to me like glue because I recognize that we often get distracted by the pain and heartache we endure and we miss the lessons. I missed plenty. And I, eventually, repeated them throughout my life, making it tougher and tougher to get out of my own way.

People may not understand the places I have been or the things I have been through and they are not supposed to. God sees and understands perfectly. For much of the journey, this life requires endurance during the storm and learning the lessons along the way so that you can move forward. Often you do this traveling alone. I know for me, I have learned things the hard way due to the repetitiveness we require. It's just human nature. It positions us to bump our heads the same way until we learn the lesson. But it causes great pain.

The ugly part of the paths we have traveled, troubles and haunts us. I often wonder if the pain could have been avoided or if I would have been spared some of the pain if I had made note of the lessons sooner. I spent so much time wondering how I came this far, but God's word tells us that tests and trials produce testimony and *that* produces healing. I believe that when you complete this book and hear about my journey, *our* journeys, you will be blessed and understand that life is about pressing forward. It will have potholes, rocks in the road, streams to cross and even broken glass. There will be smooth paths and light along the way to get through the darkest hours if we keep God with us. This life is an adventure, so "Live this Unscripted Journey!"

For I know the plans I have for you," declares the Lord, "plans to prosper you and not to harm you, plans to give you hope and a future. Jeremiah 29:11 NIV

Poem: Little Girl

Little girl, I hear you crying inside, smiling when underneath is all this pain, laughing when beneath the surface you are afraid to release to express yourself...

The relentless beating of your heart beneath your skin... the rage building inside, there's no way out of this. Underneath the surface of this woman, lies a Little Girl... Trapped, discouraged, outnumbered, emotionally triggered...

Underneath the surface of this woman, there's a fatherless child, a motherless heart, a broken spirit... Broken... Underneath the skin of this woman, there is fear, where is the hope?

Hoping, no one can see the pain trapped inside... so, she smiles... Hopefully, she can disguise the trouble that lies deep below the skin...

Above her. Over her. All around her.

The circumference of her zone, in her zone, she is continuously reminded of mistakes of the past and riddled with guilt and shame.

She whispers in the darkness, they know! There, that's where darkness exists, a battle to escape the negative thoughts I cannot hide anymore... She screams inside, at the Little Girl... Enough!

Chapter One:

Just A Little Girl

THERE SEEMS TO BE some misconception that, as women, we dream about -or in some ways are mesmerized by- the solitude of raising children alone in our quest for independence. As I grow as a mother and acknowledge this independence in the isolation of my singleness, I recall how I viewed motherhood as a child. As a little girl, I was a lover of Barbie Dolls. And every Christmas, I would have Barbies and houses and cars and all the accessories under the tree. I remember the excitement when I got my first Ken and Skipper dolls. I can recall pretending Barbie having to babysit Skipper as I played, even when Skipper had to intrude on Barbie and Ken's dates. I would find myself mimicking the kind of relationship between a mother, a father and a child that I never had. I could easily play it out and imagine the dynamic despite not having experienced it myself. I believe it was a playtime filled with love and great imagination. Especially since I did not have that dynamic for myself. It is incredible how instinctively God created us to connect. Men, women, and children, whether in a two-parent household or not, recognize that dynamic early on.

Not one time, as a little girl, however, do I ever recall envisioning Ken and Barbie creating a family and Barbie having to fare on her own or desiring to struggle in the way my mother had done. I do not believe any woman of any race, color, nationality, or creed would envision carrying the load of such an enormous responsibility alone. When I consider my childhood, I think about a time where I wanted nothing more than to be loved, hugged, and embraced by my father. I recall the same need for my mother's love, the same thirst within my heart. I could not tell you if I even had any empathetic notions that my mother's life was not happy or that we lived a disadvantaged life. We would go to the welfare office, and we had food stamps like all the families in my neighborhood. We had clean clothes and a roof over our heads, so to me, we were okay. My mother cooked three meals a day, faithfully, and we had snacks and laughter. I had her love, and she had my adoration. I was just a little girl, what else could I possibly need?

I grew up on the west side of Detroit with my mom. Our whole family lived not far from my mom and me. We lived in several places off Joy Road and I can recall them, all, very clearly. We lived in a duplex on Manor and Oakman, an apartment at Joy Road and Steele, and an apartment on Wyoming and Joy Road. I was a little girl to the core equipped with beads, barrettes, and baby dolls. In my eyes, my mother was the best mom, and she came with superpowers and magic in her food. I saw her heart and I was her biggest protector and cheerleader. Mainly, because my mother was different from the other moms and I knew that early on. She dressed differently, no dresses or pearls. And there were no men in and out of our lives. Except for Daddy, of course. I am grateful that she was always hugging and kissing and talking to me. The kids at school reminded me often just how different she was, making fun of her oversized t-shirts and jeans and lack of make-up. To confirm their thoughts, my dad never came to the school, but I did not see what they saw. I only saw love, so I defended her at all costs.

Rescued

When we moved to the apartment on Wyoming and Joy Road, some things changed about my mommy. I had to be in grade school because I remember walking with my lunch and

Alicia R. Stokes & Tyeisha L. Dalton

backpack to McFarland Elementary School. A lot of things changed in how she moved and mothered me when we moved there. She would leave for days at a time and then return and sleep for hours and hours. There were always strangers around our house and I would be left here and there, for short periods at a time, with them. I never felt like I was in danger, but now as an adult, I know that God kept me covered. It was His saving grace because anything could have happened to me. My grandparents would often have to come to my rescue, and mom would come to their house to pick me up. We were always "good" for just a little while. She was a functioning addict.

The last time my mom left me, I woke up and I was in the house all by myself. I spent the day alone and hungry. Our neighbor came and checked on me, periodically, which she was solicited to do before my mom left, I am sure. She may have left food and I do not remember if I ate. I was just crying and waiting for her. My mom always came back. Always. So, the knock at the door filled me with excitement and love and I never considered that she would have just used her key to get in. I ran to look out the window and saw my grandparents and the police. The memory here is vague. I believe a Child Protective Services worker was there, also, but after two or three days alone, I was just happy to see them.

Just like most times when they rescued me, there was so much discussion about my superhero, my mom. Ugly comments and negative things said about her that I made it a point to make a note of. I could not wait to tell her what they said when she came to get me. I was so dedicated to her, I was loyal to a fault. I had a natural child-like love for her, yet, I came in second place time after time. There was always something more important than me that kept her from me. My mother would often hurt me, emotionally. She had been in and out of rehabilitation even before I was born, but I remember going to see her one time. It was the day my Papa had his retirement celebration. He had retired from the City of Detroit, and we were going to celebrate! I was very anxious to see her and when we stopped by the rehabilitation center, I barely let the car stop before hopping out. I recall the building clearly. It was off Linwood. I recently was in that area, and memories came crashing back, so I looked it up online. It's called the Elmhurst Home. Today, it stands as a men's facility. The women's facility is in Highland Park, Michigan; still open, working to save moms and dads, too. Somehow, I found peace in that. That there is help for children growing up as I did.

The year was 1989, and I was five years old. I had gotten dressed in my pretty clothes and new shoes. After leaving the visit with my mom, my family and I danced the night away. I was missing her, but for just a moment, things were normal for me.

Homecoming

When she came home, she did well for a long while. She worked and did motherly things. It was great. Her little girl was growing up, but I was still her baby and my loyalty was to her. I wanted her to be okay so bad. Somehow, despite my best efforts in school and helping to cook, to listen and being a good girl, the addiction crept back into our lives. My mother had explained to me what her triggers were after rehab. My grandparents and family had much to do with her addiction and she had to stay away from them. Otherwise, I would be losing her to the streets. So I learned to understand her and love her more. I had compassion for her and it made me even more eager to protect her. My Papa would threaten to "take me" from her, often, and begged her to leave me with them more times than I can count. She would always say "no" and, for just a little while, we would be good. She would walk upright. I believe I was important to her. The battle she had was just more powerful than her love for me.

Alicia R. Stokes & Tyeisha L. Dalton

I Needed Her to Win

I saw my mother acquire wins in her life and I loved it! She graduated from sobriety programs and attended school for culinary arts. She worked as a Banquet Server for years and I developed a love for fine foods and food preparation, watching and helping her. Mom worked at the Ritz Carlton in Dearborn and had the privilege of preparing food for celebrities such as Prince –along with other famous people. She would come home and share her days with me and it was so amazing to see her happy, enjoying life.

I had seen my mom with money in abundance and flat broke, working hard to keep things afloat. I had witnessed her give her last to undeserving people, so selflessly and free. I was also present when she re-dedicated her life to Christ and for many years, things were going normal for us. Food, stable shelter, fishing, and cooking. We spent time together and we created memories. It was a wonderful time in my life, but just as soon as I got comfortable and relaxed, we would be back with Papa and Grandma. Our experience was rich in love, but we could not shake the darkness.

Skeletons

Mom would go on binges and I remember hearing Grandma pray for her to come back safe when women would turn up dead on the news. Often, she would return without a scratch. Other times, wrapped up in bandages, cut up and bruised. The excuses? She had them down to a science!

One day, we had borrowed Papa's car and mom decided that we should visit our old neighbors since they were standing around outside. She parked the car and I peered up at our old window feeling the memories and heartache that space held. We got out and I ran ahead hugging LB, a friend, and his mother. Suddenly, I heard yelling and I turned around. The look of terror on my mother's face is forever etched in my heart. I watched as a man lunged at her and she began to run. My mom is 4'11 and, at the time, she didn't carry much weight. She was so fast, ducking and dipping, as he tried to hit her. I had to take cover and watch her run around Papa's car. She made this man angry and he was dead-set on collecting what he told her she owed him. He chased her and she ran and ran, barely dodging his attack, for what seemed like forever.

She finally made it to the door and we hid inside LB's house, taking cover until the coast was clear. She thanked them and apologized for the drama and we headed out towards the car to leave. The man who chased my mom had continued to yell and threaten her while we were inside, but eventually he left. I guess before he left he took his anger out on Papa's car and kicked two considerably large dents on the passenger side of his Cadillac doors. I noticed the dents as we ran and hopped inside, heading back to Papa and Grandma's house. As she backed-in the driveway, she looked at me with the same fear-filled eyes, confirming another secret I knew was meant to be kept.

I stayed loyal to my mother through the drug abuse that ruled over her. She needed me, after all. Everyone else judged her and caused her to abuse drugs. I had to be a safe place for her. I had to be good and keep from triggering her, too. I was just a little girl, but I had to protect her. That is what I set out to do from then on. Even if I had to keep her secrets.

Trauma Mama

Some portions of my life are a bit of a blur for me. I believe we instinctively block trauma out for our own well-being. I learned in therapy that we suppress traumas, tucking them away in our minds defensively, as a protective measure. They are often called to memory when you endure new wounds and then you are forced to face them head-on.

My mother had two things that would impact my life as I got older and these things created triggers in my interpersonal dealings. The addiction tha she battled was one. It produced in me unhealthy loyalty and abandonment. The other is her affinity for the same gender. Or, as she explained it to me, she was gay. I will get into that in just a moment; but as I got older, she was intentional in trying to save me from her vices, from the world. I remember learning about crack cocaine and learning firsthand what a pipe was. She very clearly instructed me to not ever, never, allow anyone to give it to me to try... or any other drug for that matter. I am not sure how old I was though, maybe five or six; but I don't think I connected the dots as that being a struggle for her. I thought she was just teaching me. I understood that she was different from other mommies and I was okay with that because she was special to me.

As I mentioned, I knew when I was very young that she dated women, but I was teased about it often throughout my life. So, I denied it. There were several ladies whom I had encountered along the way. Many were super amazing to me and added to our lives. Yvonne was the cream of the crop. I remember the good ones the best, but especially Yvonne. She was my favorite as she provided love to me like I was her child. She showered me with hugs and butterfly kisses. That was our thing! She would hug me and flutter her eyelashes across my cheek. Yvonne was a part of our lives and I do not know what my mom did to ruin it. One day she just stopped coming over. My mom told me, "I messed up, I messed up bad baby" when I asked for her. I heard that before and so I knew that Yvonne was gone forever. It felt as if she left *me* and that hurt for a while.

Then there was Deborah. She was delightful and gentle and had a very calm, soft voice. And long beautiful hair. I could play in it sometimes. I remember that she used to smell like my mommy. There was this distinct smell I noticed when my mother would leave and return after several days. When I would see Deborah, sometimes she carried that odor. I know now that they had the same addiction, hence the *odor*. Crack cocaine has a very distinct smell and it would be on them both until they showered. Deborah passed away several years later, sadly enough. She was a fantastic person and her life was valuable.

Relationships

There were a few women in my mom's life that I never trusted or cared for and choose not even to mention here, but there was one unforgettable person. Unforgettable in a way that scares. She was, in fact, the worst person I had ever encountered; and, for my mom, she was just as bad as her drug addiction. Things in my life took a change when she entered it. And she was the last straw before I asked to live with my grandparents, abandoning my loyalties to my mom for good.

Bridget. She left such a mark on my life that her name is a complete sentence. I called her AB, short for Aunt Bridget. The time spent blending with AB and her family had started as a very positive thing. My mom had been 'clean' for a while when they met. She was in a culinary arts program at Breithaupt Career and Technical Center. And she somehow stumbled into a friendship journey with this woman. AB was around at the school and I suppose I was slightly blind to their interactions outside of the school. Especially since she was married with three children. They seemed to have become close friends, fast and we had begun spending time with her and her family at their home. I recall the time their friendship began since I had just been released from the hospital and AB and her family felt like a nice change.

Right before 5th grade at Warren G. Harding Middle School, I had been hospitalized for Meningitis. I spent weeks at Henry Ford Hospital. While in hospital, I remember hearing whispers that I was misdiagnosed. But I believe this was another time where God showed up and healing took place because His hands are on my life.

I realize that God has been with me for a long time, shining down and protecting me. When I think about all I had been through by the age of twelve, it was nothing but God's protection that saved me. I was fatherless, conditioned to accept -and expect- being abandoned; I was left in drug houses with sketchy people and I was never raped or tried drugs. And if that's not the definition of grace, tuh! I just know that I am grateful.

At any rate, the whole time I was at Henry Ford Hospital, I would get up and walk around visiting other children. Many of them would never make it back to their homes due to terminal illnesses; but as I recall those experiences, laughing and loving where I could, reading and talking to them, I find purpose. I have always had a love for people and I remember that I did provide that as a child. Soon, however, it was time to be released from the hospital. So there we were, mommy and I, clear of all health troubles and ready for a new adventure.

My mommy barely knew how to manage my long thick hair and I had severe bedhead from laying in the hospital all those weeks with a puffball. I begged for a relaxer the entire hospital stay and I was still asking, non-stop, up until my release. My Aunt Venae' would usually braid my hair, but I was a big girl now so braids were out of the question! I begged my mom to relax my hair and AB's oldest daughter pressured her, convincing her to let me get it done. AB applied the relaxer and I started school with my hair stretched down my back.

During the first week of school, the other girls would play in my hair as I would swing it from side to side, tossing it around. I was so happy. I was simply in love with my hair and life was leveling off. I was so pleased with my look! You could not tell me that I was not the most beautiful thing in fifth grade! Months went by and it was time for a touch-up. One day, things took a turn for the worse. Not only was my hair coming out, but something had started to make a life on my face, in the center of my nose. We thought it was acne, a breakout. But it was hard and it started to grow larger and larger. Also, no other blemishes had appeared. I picked at it one day until it bled. What a mess I had made. Some time passed and the hair damage was terrible. My Aunt Venaé told me that AB had used a super relaxer on my hair and that it was much too harsh for me. This type of relaxer was not designed for my hair such as the kiddie ones marked for my age range. So, at this point, my hair was ruined, I had this ugly brown thing on my nose, and now I was being teased in school. My life was a total nightmare. During all of this, my mom had started disappearing again. The streets called her and she had answered.

When Trouble Calls

When I look back, the addiction called much too often and my mom always answered. Eventually, she and I had to move from our house on Burt Road and it was during that transition, back and forth to my grandparents' house, that I learned the ugly thing on my nose was a wart. There was a parallelism to my life at that time. I had something "ugly" growing on the outside to match what the inside felt like.

Everything was upside down, once more, in my life. It was a terrible time. I was ten years old for crying out loud! And, as if things could not be any worse, shortly after turning eleven, my menstrual cycle began. My mom was a pretty good resource, but Aunt Tonya, her baby sister, gave me Judy

Alicia R. Stokes & Tyeisha L. Dalton

Blume's book "Are You There God, It's Me, Margaret?" It was so awesome to read about what I was going through, and it made me feel normal. My Aunt Tonya was always there for me when I needed her, like a big sister, but much bossier, *haha*. As I got older, during the dark times, she would become my covering, my safety. When you saw her, you would see me as if I were her baby.

Now here I was in school feeling terrible, appearance-wise, and being about the wart on my face. The girls who used to run their fingers through my hair now laughed that it was falling out. You just assume that everyone knows what you are facing. But even if they do not, it was exhausting, believing otherwise! When fifth grade ended, I was supposed to be looking forward to entering middle school. Instead, I was worried because mom had lost our home and we had to move out.

During that time, we had several pets. We had a rabbit, a dog, and two cats. We kept the cats, Jack and Caprice, but the dog and rabbit? I have no clue what she did with those. We moved in with mom's friend, Sherita, after that and I was between her house and my grandparents' home. Sherita and my mom had been "involved", once upon a time. I remembered her and did not care for her very much. I spent as much time at Papa and Grandma's house as I could, that summer, since my friends were on their block and Sherita's was not a comfortable place.

At this time in my life, Aunt Tonya worked in a Dermatology office. My Grandma saw to it that I got my face looked at as acne was, seemingly, the problem. As it turned out, the giant eyesore in the middle of my face could be removed. It was a simple procedure at the Dermatologist's to remove the wart. I still have the scar today. I have many scars, but this one is the one I love the most. This one removed the "ugly" on the outside. What a relief, right?

Well, Sherita and my mommy argued all the time since my mom was in the streets, again. After a while, we were put out of her home and, by this point, I was sick and tired. Why were we put out? I really couldn't tell you what went down, but the way my mom packed our things, it must have been ugly. We had to leave Jack and Caprice, my cats, behind. I was so sad leaving them. We had them since they were kittens and it was not fair that I had to keep losing things I valued. They were my babies and, to me, I was abandoning them. Throughout the years, I had lost so much. It was almost second nature, by now. So I brushed it off. Sherita was supposed to look after them, but one day we went by her place to see them. I learned that they supposedly "ran" out the door when she opened it and they were gone. I never, not for a second, believed they just ran out. The funny thing is, I was always punished for adult problems. I am sure that the woman let them out due to her distaste for my mom. That happens, you know. We make our children victims of our mistakes and circumstances. I had to endure another loss.

Auntie Venae' started braiding my hair again and it was growing fast. Just imagine heading to the sixth grade with French braids, feeling *ugly* all over again. The ugly was the start of an internal battle with my self-esteem. I understand this now as an adult. My confidence was tied to what I looked like. There was no one I can recall reminding me or telling me that I was beautiful and amazing. Not one person. If you factor in all the funny looks and teasing from other kids to what I felt on the inside, it all took a toll on me. The dust had begun to settle in our lives and we were waiting to move into a new house with AB and her family. AB was getting divorced and we would benefit from cohabitating with them, but I knew better and I did not immediately agree that this would be a great option. However, my mom seemed to be doing better, so I was hopeful. In addition, it was officially time to prepare for middle school. The end of summer would make that final. So here we were, less than a year later, on a new adventure. The

Alicia R. Stokes & Tyeisha L. Dalton

kids on our block were super "ghetto" and nothing like the ones I grew up with on Papa and Grandma's block. At my grandparents' house, I grew up riding bikes and having discussions about college and dreams with neigbors such as the Brooks family and my friend Patrice, God rest her soul. She has since transitioned, along with the head of the Brooks household, and thier home sits empty now.

I have many good memories of my childhood, but moving in with AB, was not one of them. It was here when I had my introduction to mean girls. Most members of this family were bullies. Mean and evil people…from parents down to the youngest child. And to make matters worse, I did not get along with AB's niece that she was raising with her other children. I shared a room with the niece and, during this time, I learned to stay to myself. Her youngest son and I, however, were super tight, but I was still the *outsider* when they all got together against me. Still, he and I would dance and rap and be silly. He was my favorite and still is today, my brother. He was the best part of the whole time with them and I love him.

AB's niece would disrupt my space and go into things my Grandma bought me. My mommy never listened when I complained about it. Well, she may have heard me, but she never gave any supporting action. I would tell my Grandma, and she would get on my mother for leaving me uncovered. That would hold things off for a short time. I wonder now, though, why would you have to remind someone to protect their offspring from another person? It is beyond my understanding.

One time, the niece caught me when I was in a bad mood and we got into a scuffle over my things. I was simply tired of her and the disrespect, so I cornered her and I punched her a few times, pushed her, and rushed to tell my mom my side thinking things would be okay. Boy, was I wrong! Per usual, I got in trouble, but this time my mom told me to go into the basement and wait for her. I had a few butterflies, and I was uncertain as to why there was a need to go down there to talk about this, but I went. She came downstairs soon after with a belt in her hand. I was so shocked. I had already been crying since she didn't offer any understanding or aid and now there we were, looking at one another, and I was certainly not about to get the support I was after. She whooped me! Can you believe that? She had the nerve to discipline me. Me? Her only child. In 11 years, I had never gotten a whooping because I was a good kid. Heck, I was a great kid! I never got into trouble, I never talked back. Well, I did, but I was smart enough to whisper it under my breath so she didn't hear it. I was appalled and furious that she would go against me, again, and it was the final straw. She never took up for me or even came to my rescue anymore and as I looked down, I noticed through the tears that I was bleeding from my hand. The buckle caught my hand. At that moment, I was numb to the pain and to her. My mother. Would I even believe that is what she was anymore?

I stayed quiet for days and endured a lot of verbal abuse and threats from the other children as we came and went for school, along with other moments when my mother was not present. Remember AB's oldest daughter that talked her into relaxing my hair? She was the biggest issue for me. She would corner me and say mean things and jump at me like she was going to hit me. I was the outsider and as soon as I got the chance, I told my Grandma during a visit that I did not want to live with them. My mother was back chasing her addiction, again, and I was even more exposed to their exclusions. My mom was in love with the new family she had found, so I left and never looked back. Papa and Grandma eventually became my guardians since AB convinced my mother not to allow them to adopt me. Once it was all over, it was never the same between us, my mother and me.

Alicia R. Stokes & Tyeisha L. Dalton

That's Still Your Mama/Daddy

There are things a little girl needs from a mother that I simply did not get after a certain age. Defeated in the daughter department. Looking back over my life, yes, at 11, I was considering my past. I was so unhappy and alone. I was mature for my age and fed up with life, altogether. I was quiet and determined to do well in school so I could get far away from it all, but I did not desire to be "grown". I wanted to be free from Detroit and my life there, as a whole. I learned at a young age what love is *not* supposed to feel like. And I was determined about what it was going to be and feel like as I grew up. Reflecting on this time in my life, I realize how the constant abandonment changed my views on love. I loved my mother, she was my superhero. That love was always there even after being angry with her. I still recognized it, but as the years went on and the sadness increased, the love began to get lost and covered by bitterness and anger. That child-like love turned into resentment and pain. I had to close my heart and not allow myself to feel. After all, I was headed to middle school now, and there was no room for that love and baby stuff.

I entered Brooks Middle School in 1996 and I did well. I had always done well in school. I remember stepping and dancing. I sang at school events and I was on the Step Team. I guess you could say that I was a "cool kid". You know, relatively active. Also, I had friends. However, I still possessed an emptiness within me, despite my social life and ability to fit in. As well, I had a grandma doing all that she could to fill in the blanks. I was getting by at this stage and I was used to not talking to anyone about my feelings. Not having a mother, not having a daddy, it was all my normalcy. My grandparents did all they could to make life level-out for me. For my twelfth birthday, I got Buttons, my best friend! He was a poodle that my grandparents surprised me with and I was so convinced that things were turning around at this point. I had what I needed and most of what I wanted, so I never longed for anything material.

Of course, just as soon as I thought I was in the clear and emotionally in control, here comes Larry Green... deciding he wants to be a daddy in the third quarter of the game. From my grandparetns, I was used to hearing, "that's still your mama" and now the tide turned to "that's still your daddy" seeing as I wanted nothing to do with him. I was tired of the emptiness, but I had adjusted to not having him in my life. Thanks, but no thanks!

Alicia R. Stokes & Tyeisha L. Dalton

Poem: Those Damn Daddy Issues

So, I've always wondered what it would be like to have him...

I imagined waking up to his smiling face, fixing him burnt toast and eggs, making a silly picture, buying a tie for Father's Day, and the infamous ride on his shoulders...

Yeah, I bet that is awesome... It is a faint and distant memory of a little girl turned into a woman with daddy issues...

Daddy issues, yeah, that's it Those Damn Daddy Issues!

You must dig deep to understand...I've been that girl, the one who was overlooked. I've been the one who was shy, and quiet, you know the "nerd". I've been that girl pretending to be doing "it," whatever "it" was because "it" was cool...

I've been that girl holding on to what I thought was the worst pain ever, No daddy...

No one to love me and lead me away from men who meant me no good...

No one to spoil me so I wouldn't be fooled by flashy gifts and things...

He died in 2012; emptiness settled in...

I finally visited his gravesite...

I poured my heart out to him, right there... The love I had for him stronger than ever pouring out with each drop. But how?

His headstone reads "loving husband". The absence of his title as a "loving father" was clear in death just as it was in life in my eyes...

I'd been chasing this man, my daddy, all my life...

Now stationary in this grave, he couldn't run from me anymore...

He couldn't pull off when he saw me coming, he had to listen to me and feel the weight of my existence as a result of his absence...I had it bad, Those Damn Daddy Issues...

MY MONOLOGUE: Having "daddy issues" created in me a *thing* for those men, the older ones who meant me no good. Men half my age. Men I chased just like I chased my daddy.

It started in 1999 with Omar. He was fine! He worked in the Operating Room at the hospital I worked at for the summer. He was 28 years old. At 12 years old, I was just a baby, but we talked on the phone. He gave me compliments and butterflies.

Then there was Dejuan. He was 18 when I was 16 and we talked on the phone all night. We even snuck to the movies without anyone knowing where I was. We shared light kisses. Everything crashed down on me when Grandma found a letter I wrote expressing my love and adoration for him in my pants, as she did laundry, and that was that.

Now, before Dejuan, there was George. He was my first real love in high school. He was 18 and I was 14. I didn't forget him…he was just special. He was my first real kiss and we almost did "it". He left after high school without a real discussion and broke my heart. That was the 2nd heartbreak I experienced. Daddy still reigns as the #1 champ.

After all that, I still managed to dodge the slippery, sneaky boys all throughout high school! They could not trick me into losing my precious virginity with their immature and sly ways. Nope, NOT ME!

And then there was college. Now in college, the game changed. It's on a different level. It's more advanced with more mature guys, but I dodged those moments, too!

Then one summer I came home and met *him*. This one, he was the one who gave me the real *firsts*. First motorcycle ride, first lesson in intimacy, first… well, EVERYTHING! Even a baby. He was 23 and I was 18. He was beautiful to me, I loved his hustle, his creativity, and his mind. He stimulated me in conversation and we both loved music. More butterflies. He introduced me to pleasure. And then came the pain…PAIN. You know, "After the paaaain" Betty Wright sang it best!

Alicia R. Stokes & Tyeisha L. Dalton

By my 20th birthday, I was in love, no longer a virgin and my Princess Iyana was on the way. My belly was growing and growing. I was pregnant and alone. He was gone despite the ideas he poured into me of "family" and talks of me being his wife. He stamped my passport BABY MAMA and exited.

It was my decision to be pro-choice. In my unwillingness to abort the mission, I lost the position. But see, I had this thing for those older men. In all their masculinity and fatherly ways...

It was Those Damn Daddy Issues...

There I stood an educated black woman, successful in my own right, but not to *me*. Broken and filled with "shoulda, coulda, woulda's" I was convinced that there was something wrong with me because everything failed. I wasn't able to identify it until I got the news of his death. My daddy. He died and I was a mess. I was lost and empty. I had so much on my chest so much love to give. I had much forgiveness to achieve. Time is short so I must find value. Now I sit at his grave with regrets and...

Those Damn Daddy Issues play on repeat...

I know what you are thinking. One should be able to get on with life, suck it up, stop blaming others for their mistakes, time (presumably) heals wounds and blah, blah, blah. Okay, fair enough. But *Those Damn Daddy Issues* are real! They haunt the woman with the girl inside that craves his protection. The cycle must be broken and daddies should be there to build-up their princesses. To love her so good that no one could fool her if they tried. Other men should never add up to him. It should be an unreachable bar. For me, the bar was never set...
Those Damn Daddy Issues

Chapter Two:

Daddy Issues

MY FATHER, LIKE MOST absent fathers from our generation, decided when he wanted to be involved and when he did not. I would see him often and when I saw him, I chased him. Well, what do you mean you chased him, Tyeisha? I shared that most of my life my father lived near my mother and I so I would see him when we were out walking. At the liquor store, getting ice cream, and even at the grocery store. I remember one time, skating down Joy Road with my mother and I spotted his car. I started to skate towards his car and I could see him at the payphone booth in his Cadillac, so I took off. I looked both ways and crossed Meyers, a busy intersection leaving my mother behind yelling for me to be careful. As I got closer, he saw us and floored it! I got to the payphone where the handset was just swinging back and forth and I cried. I swallowed the pain and looked at my mother. She always embraced me and she never uttered a bad word about my daddy. This incident was the first of many occasions where I would shed tears on the chase…chasing my Daddy. He only ran sometimes. You know, when we would see him out and about in our neighborhood. He would visit our house occasionally, but always without any financial support for my mom or anything I needed and surely never any gifts. I am not sure I remember exactly when I met him for the first time, but the one visit I recall, he sat and talked with me. I asked him, "Daddy, why don't you come and see me"? I would always ask him questions, and he would say something obnoxious. He answered the question in typical fashion, saying, "your mom will not let me move in!". This response hit me differently. It irritated and hurt me, so I asked him to leave through the front door that I held open and just like that, he was gone. I was about four years old and there were minimal encounters in our home after that.

Memories are what make life special. They can be happy, sad, or upsetting. You remember them when you least expect. Perhaps through a dream or as a sudden thought crosses your mind. And there it is. It can be haunting or feel like an awakening, jarring you right to a place or space in time that we would like to forget. We often spend time trying to erase memories when they evoke pain, reminding us of where we have been, or the broken pieces and places in our hearts. Those places are where forgiveness can be found, where you must learn to press forward to win. That's where we hope memories take us. I am not sure I understood *winning*. It seems like you just take what you can get. And if it happens to be a win, then you go on.

Fast-forward to 1998, I was excited to be preparing for my freshman year in high school. And Middle School graduation was approaching. But the eighth-grade dance was first. I had a pretty orange dress that Grandma had purchased for me and, for the moment, my dad was working on being an active participant in my life. Daddy came and picked me up in a limo. I was delighted as we headed to pick up Norman, my date. I danced and had a blast with my friends and, once it was over, daddy told me he wanted to take me somewhere. He promised me a ride in the limo, so we took off! We ended up making several stops where he made sure that I met my older brother and some of my sisters. I immediately fell in love with Carnel, my eldest brother. From the moment we met, we were joined at the hip and he was determined to be there for me.

Carnel was my biggest supporter and is, still, everything to me! He dedicated so much time listening to me and asking about my feelings. He showed genuine love and care for me. We would watch old videos of my dad singing and he gave me the scoop, from his perspective, on some of what I'd missed growing up without our father. I am grateful for those times with my brother and I am not sure he truly knows the magnitude of love I have for him. I would not trade those years, ever, even though they still held so much pain from my dad. I secretly held jealousy that Carnel and my other siblings had pieces I would never be able to relate to. Fragments of Daddy that, to this day, are missing for me. An emptiness that may never correctly be filled.

Ray Vs. Larry

Growing up, my mother always referred to my father as Larry and this was what I always thought his name was. He would come to visit me at my grandparent's house, periodically, for family functions and just to talk to my Grandma. I remember one day that he came by, he told me he wanted to speak to me. We sat down in the living room and he broke the news to me that I had a baby brother. He wanted us to meet, but he would have to make it appear as if he was coming by to pick up money for a limo rental. He was worried about us being so close in age that we would begin dating, so he brought him by only a few times and that was that.

Learning about my baby brother was interesting. My dad seemed to be a bit frantic. His spirit seemed heavy as he told me about my baby brother. But I was distraught. I now went from being an only child to having five sisters and two brothers. I still felt such an empty feeling inside even though I would like to believe that I was embraced by them, all.

It was odd meeting people for the first time at the funeral of my eldest sister. She passed away a few years after my dad introduced me to everyone. I was just in an awkward place and, in a sense, still being *hidden* in plain sight. Though it did not last long. Soon after I met my brother, we got a visit from my dad's wife. She was "kind" enough to bring his social security number, full name, and other information so my Grandma could put him on child support. I was troubled by this new information. After all this time, another lie. My father's name was Ray Green. Not Larry, despite the years of thinking this was who he was.

My dad and his current wife, my baby brother's mom, were divorcing and he wanted us to meet so that we would not run into one another and possibly date. We were introduced, but not as siblings immediately. And, as I think back, I can laugh now. At the time, it was rather disturbing, the deception, right? It was torture as I thought back to all the years of being avoided and hidden behind the scenes. It was just a crappy feeling.

It took me to a time when we pulled up to my father's family house in southwest Detroit. We got out and I guess they all knew I was coming because there were tons of people on the porch. We approached a woman who I know now as his mother, my paternal grandmother. My father said to her, "this my daughter, Tyeisha". She looked at me for a minute and said to him, "Another one? How do you know this one, yours?" He grabbed my hands and showed them to her. I would not go so far as to say proudly, just as an assurance. You see, I was like my father who was born with an extra finger. Well, for me, one on each hand. So, in a way, I was branded just as he was. Now understand, this is the only memory I have of this woman and I have never forgotten it. I never even saw her again after that visit.

I remember countless times seeing my father. You remember the chase? Well, one of those times he was with my sister, who appeared to be close to my age. I ran up on his car near Joy Road and Wyoming like always and saw her. I wondered why they were so lucky, allowed to be with him and experience his love. He wanted them and not me. Why? Why not me? These are questions to which I will never have answers, but the assumption is because I was the only one born outside of his marriages. I was the one, unspoken child. A reminder of at least one of his acts of infidelity. The magnitude of shame I carried from being unwanted was deep. Being unwanted leaves you to question everything about life...who you are, who you will be. The high self-esteem that should have been instilled in me while I was growing up, I never received. It was never poured into me. Even if it was offered, the issues I faced were no match for that kind of love. I always felt like I had to accept what I could get and I believe that, subconsciously, this followed me into the next chapter of life in a life-altering way. I will never have answers and I just must move forward. Right?

Baby Brother

I had siblings and I was two months older than my baby brother. This startling revelation did not scar our relationship. Surprisingly, my baby brother and I became tight when we met. My baby brother, and I, locked in. So much so, that he helped celebrate my sweet 16. He was a part of my special day and my dad even brought my cousins from his side of the family that were around my age. I later went to homecoming with my brother and we talked, laughed, and loved on one another. It was a great memory, but unfortunately, that did not last. Life lead us on different paths. We walked our inidividual paths and my father's death would bring us together again in 2012. Now, we love from afar. Somewhere during that time, after our meeting, his mother found out about me and came by to "make it right". She dropped off my father's real name and his social security number for child support, I suppose. Now let me guess, you missed that last part, I grew up believing my father was Larry Green. I learned his name is Ray Green and I was immediately empty again. All this time, a lie? A lie he catered and nurtured with a casual smile. How much can one girl take? No closer to knowing who I am and now another betrayal. My life throughout this time had been dark and no one knew, but

I was not willing to lose, so I decided on my plan of escape and I set out to build a life that would never mirror what I'd encountered. My dad was "around", but I wanted nothing to do with him. As I got older, there were lots of shocking details about him that produced anger inside. Like finding out that he lived between 5-8 blocks away from me most of my life and failed to father me.

<u>Papa's Girl</u>

From the day I was born, they tell me I was always Papa's girl. I always felt his love. I know he loved me. I can close my eyes, at times, and vividly feel the impression of love he left with me. All the time I spent chasing my biological father for love and adoration. But my Grandpa was always there. My Papa, as I called him, was so loving and it was amazing to listen to him and laugh. Did I tell you he was amazing? Well, I know that was extra, but he was there for everything and took me whenever and wherever I needed throughout high school and my first job at *The Finish Line*. With my Papa there, it didn't matter that my daddy wasn't around. Well, not that much. I will always remember Willie B. Dalton, Sr. His laugh, his love. His presence in my life through the completion of college will be with me forever.

He protected me for as long as I could remember. One time I had been out with my mother on one of her binges and we got to my grandparents' house. There was arguing since they had not heard from us in days and my Papa asked my mom to just leave me with him. He would tell her this often, despite and, despite that, I still felt abandoned. This particular visit my mom had made him so upset that Papa asked me to come to him and he hugged me, ensuring I was okay. I think back to missing and wanting my father so badly, but Papa had filled those shoes. Even if my father did not wish to love me, Papa always did. And he wanted the best for me.

I had a small hair box with all my barrettes and beads. It was black and red plaid and I took it EVERYWHERE we went. Beads and braids were my staple hairdo. One of the places we would often stay, the lady would braid my hair, so I had to keep it with me. My mother made sure I was presentable. Add *that* to the list of responsible parent activities. At any rate, that box was the one constant thing in my life and we, my box and I, had seen more than a child should see. Aware of these things, Papa popped it open, took a marker, and he wrote "Dady" and the phone number to their house. I know it was spelled wrong, but it was unique and it was his way of protection. Several years ago, I found that little red and black box in a closet at their house. It was so numbing. A joyful hurt I felt inside as I recall sitting with this box countless times needing to dial his number and not being able to.

My mother and I would never be far from Papa and Grandma's house. We would be two or three blocks away from their home in either direction. So it chills me to think, had I known, I would have walked there plenty of times to escape. I mentioned that my mom had periods of "being clean". It is unclear for me in the early years, I guess grade school age, how or when she would not be affected by drug addiction. My mom had a battle, and I would never have imagined the impact it would have on our relationship. I was with my Papa and Grandma off and on for most of my adolescent years; and then 6th grade through college, it was permanent.

I remember one day we walked out of my Papa and Grandma's house. My mother was angry with them about one thing or another; this was a pattern. She would leave for days at a time and when she returned, they would forge a verbal attack and mom would get angry and leave. Usually, she would leave alone, depending on how she felt. She would drag me with her, at other times. This one time, we went two blocks from their house to her friend's apartment. We entered the home after being buzzed in and we were greeted by a male.

Alicia R. Stokes & Tyeisha L. Dalton

They exchanged pleasantries. There were others there. Several people. Men and women.

There was a couch with a tv in the middle of the room. The apartment was clean. It looked lived in, but there was no sign of any children. My mother said the famous "Sit here, I will be back" line so there I sat, uncomfortably. Now the argument with Grandma and Papa was terrible and I imagine it must have pushed her buttons because I had been sitting for what felt like hours. My patience with her was thin by this time. I was a kid and she disrupted my playtime with my friends. I was also tired of her antics, but I sat for a little while longer. Then, restlessness settled in and I was done waiting. I got up since everyone was in the bedroom and busted in the door. There she was. A pipe, lighter and all, in her hand and I froze.

I was stunned and angry and curious, but I had been teased enough by this point in my life to know that she was what "they" (the kids at school) called her…a crackhead. Of course, she never fit that description in my heart. She was always clean and would be a mommy for a while, so I was very disappointed. The sadness in her face and the hurt look in her eyes was strong but no match for mine in that moment, I am sure. I looked around at the sad, surprised faces in the room and no one else seemed to care about what I saw. My mother, she appeared broken. Defeated even. I did not even close the door behind me when I walked out. I went and sat angrily on the couch. She emerged from the room soon after and we left. I have never told anyone about this. I guess I was too ashamed to say it out loud. I was so used to the disappointment I didn't even cry. It was not the last battle coming face to face with her addiction, but I can confidently say that it was a new level of disappointment for me. I had seen too much. My Papa and Grandma were my sanctuary and being there with them was best.

Poem: Unscripted Emotion

Emotionally drained and scripted into pretending that the alignment of dysfunction is perfection. Realizing the days are shorter and the people are more significant, a vast misconception of our existence. Forcing a smile through the sunshine and crying through the rain. Soggy eyes filled with pride yet relentlessly battling to the top of the charts. Corruption in the pit and love in the clouds intertwined and emerged in bliss. A tight fist of fury torn and tattered bruised and bloodied. Blot out the traffic and resist the grip. Focus, Focus, and Breathe through the pain. Playfully wrestling for the little piece of truth... The nectar from the fruit is sweet and bitter and sour and tart yet fulfilling. Return to the original form, the unalterable form that no one can release. Build and build and build till no one, oh no one, can clear the wall...

Unscripted Emotion- your story may not have a happy beginning, but that does not determine the ending.

Chapter Three:

Entering Motherhood

IN JULY OF 2002, I headed to Michigan State University (MSU) early, as a participant of the M.A.G.I.C. program: *Maximizing Academic Growth in College*. The program aims to prepare incoming students to succeed in college. It was an excellent opportunity to get my footing and become more familiar with college life. The program is for black and brown students and it was very cool to meet new people early on. There were Hispanic students, Pacific Islanders, and of course, Black students. I noticed that there was a division amongst us. During the day, we would mingle and share space. A melting pot. But once there was free time, everyone gravitated to the people they identified with most. That was the case during all four years of college, for me.

    The diversity was not new to me. Being in the presence of people who did not look like me was second nature now. Cranbrook had prepared me for that each summer I spent on campus for the Upward Bound Program. I had been fortunate in that my Grandma made sure that I experience so much. Thinking back now, it was better to get the educational value of the programs she fought hard to place at my feet than going clubbing. I still wanted to go where my peers were going. Many of my high school friends and peers were going to St. Andrews and hanging out on the weekends. I was usually at home or had company over. Until I became friends with Shari. Then, I was often at her house.

    The independence that college offered was so freeing, especially for a girl that was sheltered much of high school. In reality, Grandma prepared me and kept me safe and focused on my studies. I graduated high school with honors. Now college was exciting and liberating and I had to work hard to stay on track. I met so many dope people that summer, including Jhamal, Iyana's godfather. I forged so many great friendships. Lindsey was my favorite. The summers I mentioned at Cranbrook, she was there too; and she was and is, still, such a beautiful person. We were roommates at M.A.G.I.C. since she had been accepted to MSU as well. Iit was comforting having a familiar face.

We had a whole tribe of mentors while we were there: Keith, Misty, Raven, Mike, and Tish. They took to us and treated us like little sisters. These people shaped how I entered college and I am forever grateful to them. Ohana means family! That was how we referred to one another and I am tied to each of these individuals, forever. That week at M.A.G.I.C., they each played a role in my journey; talking to us about college life, scheduling classes, and, most of all, preparing us for campus life. Before entering college, my mother had been sentenced to time in prison, so the extra guidance was invaluable.

Now, concerning college. I took the fun road and it landed me on academic probation during my freshman year. Grandma was furious, she was so disappointed. I was too, but I had a great time! I laugh at it now, recalling all the partying I did Thursday to Sunday, but I had to decide to get more serious with my studies because going home, back to Detroit was not an option! For my sophomore year, I scheduled all my classes early in the morning since I am an early bird. Grandma made sure I had resources at my disposal and signed me up for Kaplan tutoring to help with studying. She was committed to my education, and she pushed and pushed me. My daddy was still up to his antics; promising me the sun, moon, and the stars but not coming through for things such as books I needed for classes and things like that. I just made mental notes on that behavior and avoided his calls. My Grandma and my godmother, Mrs. Breakfield, made sure I had what I needed. It was easy to keep the distance between Daddy and me. My mom was still in prison and I felt numb. All the poor choices and decisions she made due to her addiction had caught up to her. So, as I watched other people lean on their moms and dads, I still spent most of my time solo pretending I was okay.

The Hunt

I went home that summer. I was at Circuit City with Grandma and Mrs. Breakfield getting a new computer and preparing to go back to school when I met him. Iyana's dad. I didn't officially *meet* him. I just *encountered* him. My friend, Kinshasha, worked there and that's how our paths crossed. I had playfully said something to him over her headset, and that was that.

The salesman loaded our car and said to me in a very fatherly way, "You are a beautiful young woman, God didn't design you to be a huntress". I was so confused, and I asked him to clarify what he meant. He told me that people are not what they seem to be and that I should watch the company I keep. I had no clue how to take the message, so I smiled and nodded and got in the car. A few days passed and Shari asked me to go with her to see someone. It turned out to be Iyana's uncle she was meeting and I had to run interference with his brother. That was how it all began.

To give them privacy, we talked in the basement of their mom's house. I was very timid and quiet, so the conversation was minimal. He asked if I wanted to go for a ride and I agreed. We rode downtown with music carrying us. That was the connection, a love for music, and the conversation flowed freely from there. He asked several questions about me and I missed the chance to ask anything since I was mesmerized by him. He was cute and he had a laid-back vibe. I knew he was twenty-three and headed to college at the end of the summer.

I should have walked away then. He was moving to Florida and that should have been my cue. Instead, we ended up in a relationship. The distance was not much of a factor.

My new beau and his brother, they visited us on campus. Shari, Jasmine, Deandrea and I were roommates in college, living in Holmes Hall. On one of his visits we were walking from the parking lot after he had arrived. We started talking about marriage and families and I asked if he wanted children. He said, "Yeah, I want another kid". We were about five months into this relationship and I had felt as if a bomb just dropped, which led me to ask more questions. I learned he was married but separated. And he is a father. The visit was very awkward and ended with me believing that he was going to get a divorce soon. I was left to decide if I wanted to move forward.

Junior year was due to begin and Shari and I decided we were ready to move, no longer living in the dorms. We headed to housing and signed up to moved into Spartan Village. The sememster began and we were in our first apartment. We did very well living together growing and maturing, having fun experiences. My grandmother and god mother purchased my first car, it was 2004 Since spring break was coming up we planned a trip to Florida. By this time, Shari and Iyana's uncle had split-up and I was still bright-eyed over Iyana's dad; so, the plan was to go to Tallahassee where he lived. During college I danced on URBAN DREAMS, a multicultural Hip-Hop Dance Team on campus and we had our final perfomace right before spring break. We hopped on a plane and landed safely, I was welcomed with a loving embrace. I decided then I would continue to be patient. I was smitten with this man. Shari and I were there a week and I got to meet his friends and see the school he attended. We, also, enjoyed the nightlife together. We had a great time until Shari and his roommate fell-out and I guess the time had drawn to a close for us to leave. It was a bit strained. I left Florida as I arrived, a virgin. And I was committed to that, especially since he was married. He made promises to visit ofte, and he assured me that he loved me. The divorce would be final and marriage was in our future, so I was settled in my emotions. I bought it hook, line, and sinker.

Mama's Baby, Daddy's Maybe

My Grandpa and Grandma purchased my first car. It was a 2002 Ford Focus and I was excited! They drove it up to school for me. They always took care of me. My Grandma was very hands-on, teaching me the ins-and-outs of credit and how to build-up mine. We went out and fully furnished my one-bedroom apartment. I was, as they say nowadays, living my best life! I had worked so hard to be successful and I was determined to make my family proud. I cared as to how they saw me as well as about keeping a certain image. Failing was out of the question.

I was home for Christmas break when I learned that I was carrying Iyana. I had returned, early, after a terrible visit to Florida to see her dad. He was finally divorced and I was no longer a virgin. We fought and fought, during this visit. Fights about him leaving me at his apartment for hours at a time, during the day. Supposedly, he was working, but when I called the store he worked at they would never give him the phone. The day before I left, we had a terrible argument and he made it clear that the age difference and distance was now a problem. I knew it was someone else, another woman. I was young but not stupid by a long shot. A woman had answered the phones when I called his dorm phone, so I knew the game. I was not much of a communicator then, so I wrote him a letter expressing how I felt. That is what made him angry and, so, I booked an early flight home and spent Christmas listening to The Emotions "What Do the Lonely Do at Christmas" on repeat.

At home, my family noticed my mood, but my friend DeAndrea was the only one I confided in at the time. I was feeling as sick as I had been in Florida. DeAndrea brought a pregnancy test over and I took it. Iyana's dad was in town as a surprise a month earlier, so the possibility of being pregnant was real. I was terrified as I waited and, finally, we looked at the test. The result was positive. I was devastated. There was no sound and there were no tears. I was broken. I called her dad to tell him the news and all hell broke loose. It was clear that he had no plans on having a baby with me. Not now, at least. He told me, "get rid of this one and we can have another one later." I was alone and the worst part was that I had to tell my family.

I sat with my Grandma and my Aunt Cindy told them. The look of disappointment was like a death stare. She and Aunt Cindy began looking for abortion clinics. I was infuriated and sad and I had to get out of there. I packed my car and drove back to Lansing to figure out life for myself. I searched for abortion clinics and prayed. All I could hear were the lies about the family he told me we would have, his promises to me. The craziest thing is he said to me -in detail- what this little girl he envisioned us having looked like and it stuck with me. I worked to push that from my mind and I found a clinic that was near campus and went there. I remember debating about the right thing to do and it all seemed selfish. I couldn't drink, I had not lived life or traveled and he did not want this baby. I was so torn, but I scheduled the appointment.

Game Changer

Despite several positive tests, it was clear that I was pregnant. The clinic I selected turned out to be a pro-life organization and they gave positive resources to encourage keeping the baby. They performed an ultrasound based on the date I gave them. I should have been just shy of being eight

Alicia R. Stokes & Tyeisha L. Dalton

weeks pregnant. Nothing. They found nothing. The blood test was positive. Five store-bought and in-office tests later, pregnant and no baby could be seen on their ultrasound. I had to wait a few weeks and go back. Until then, I had a great time working to put it aside. I lived and traveled with DeAndrea and Shari. There was no way I could be a mother. I was just not ready. Jhamal was kind enough to go with me (my big brother from another mother) to the scheduled final visit. He never shamed me or anything; he was, simply, a friend who supported me. By the end of the appointment, I was a mess and had a photo of my little peanut. From there, the clinic helped with her nursery and clothes which was a blessing. I decided to have my baby, and all I knew was that I would be better for her than what I had encountered.

I stayed in Spartan Village most of my pregnancy, and when my lease was up, it was time to find more space for the baby. At the end of the summer my friend, Terika, and I moved to Okemos to have more space for the kids and to be a support to one another. We lived a floor apart in the same building and the independence was easy for me. Nevertheless, I was scared preparing for a baby alone. The resources I had successfully acquired made things a smooth transition and MSU had support for moms that was helpful. We had so much lined up and since Terika had Kahmi first, I was able to have guidance. It was a blessing.

Iyana was named by Aunt Tonya when I learned her gender. And despite the strain between Grandma and me, Iyana is her namesake. Her dad was not nice to me at all while I was pregnant, so I had learned to stay to myself. It was very lonely carrying her, but I believe it helped toughen my skin. I needed to toughen up. The adventure ahead would require it.

August 30, 2005

August 30, 2005 is the day my life changed forever. I had to mature overnight as I spent my twenty-first birthday practicing nursing my baby and recovering from a cesarean surgery. I had entered my senior year at MSU that month and life was changing rapidly. Can you imagine that? Before I could legally drink, go to a bar or anything adult-like, I was a mother. I remember walking around campus all junior year and throughout the summer with a cloud of shame hovering over me. Everyone knew my secret because I was huge! I laugh now remembering skipping class to eat or sleep due to being so tired, but I survived my shame and my grades were terrific!

I was not always happy during my time carrying her and I often spent time alone, as I mentioned earlier. I do recognize that God kept me and things went so smoothly where my academics were concerned. I never had to consider leaving school. One of my Professors gave me a research opportunity that I could do from home when Iyana was born and I attended classes in the summer all four years, so I was ahead. I bet you are waiting for me to explain where I could have possibly found shame or not have been proud of myself? Well, it was all on my mind. I received so much negativity from Iyana's father and his family. As well as people who knew me as the "good girl". Being pregnant was damaging to my "image" and I was getting advice that was so discouraging. I was rightfully angry and afraid to press forward, caring way too much about what others thought of me. It was tearing me apart. However, Terika and I had built a strong foundation for our friendship during this time. She was such a great ally. All of my sister-friends were.

The pregnancy was rough on my body and I was very sick most days because I was unable to keep down any foods except French fries. Yes, French fries. And, only the frozen variety! I had a freezer full of all cuts of frozen potatoes. If you can name the style of French fries, I had them! From wedges to crinkle cut, waffle fries, and shoestrings. I often went to appointments alone unless Jhamal or Terika could go. They both were a great support for me and that is why I made them Iyana's godparents. Around the third-month things got better, physically. I was able to eat and feel "normal" again. My new normal. I made up for lost time eating everything under the sun and forcing myself to be happy. I had a pretty sound set of friends that kept me motivated. The support was real.

I was a dancer when I got pregnant with Iyana and I held the title of Public Relations Director for Urban Dreams. This was the best Hip-Hop Dance team on campus! So, there I was 121 pounds dancing with a flat stomach when I found out I was pregnant. Everything was expanding and my body was taking on a different shape, but I danced until I was about two or three months pregnant and showing. With exercise out the window, my little princess was six pounds when she was born. I was a whopping 185 pounds and huge. Looking back, she was worth it. It was all worth it because she forced me to grow up in ways I may not have grown, without her. As much as the pregnancy stunned me and those around me, Iyana was necessary to my life, my growth.

The Next Level

In 2006 I was off to Paris, France. Most of my friends that crossed the graduation stage with me had also crossed the "burning sands" and joined sororities and fraternities. They were also heading to other states to begin new work opportunities. I always wanted to pledge, but life happened and I had to set that aside. With everything on my plate, I hadn't lined up any options. The next best thing was going abroad, so I left behind my then-ten month-old baby and reassured myself that I could still press through life and make my own rules.

GRACEFULLY BROKEN: A JOURNEY OF SELF-DISCOVERY

It was the toughest six weeks of my life being away from Iyana. I talked to her on the phone, but she seemed to be mad at me and would not stay on the phone for a long time. Imagine being in one of the most beautiful places in the world with feelings of sadness. I did not enjoy being there until about a week and a half into the trip. I studied Organizational Communication at Cite' Universitaire. We also traveled to Belgium, Antrepern, and explored several businesses in Paris. It was the first time in ten months I had to prepare only for myself and in some strange way I began to see life much clearer. I had gotten lost in being a mommy so quickly that I did not even realize the importance o fseperating who I was a a person and who I was becoming as a mother.

It was a fantastic opportunity in a beautiful place and things were making sense again. Paris was a total melting pot and there were no color lines amongst the people. Nightlife was exciting and fun and we danced we explored the city. I was free of my scars and fear for a little while, so I began to relax and breathe it all in. The experience taught me that there is so much to do in this life and it changed how I viewed people. Also, I learned to embrace the moments. I would sit outside most nights or lay on a blanket and gaze into the sky. Especially during my last week there. During the final week, I was grateful for the opportunity but fearful of what the road ahead would hold. At this point in my journey, I had grown accustomed to fear, living in it and feeling comfortable. It was time to return home. My baby needed me and I had to shift gears and refocus my energy.

I spent the next few years still feeling my way through this life, working retail jobs with little fulfillment, until 2007 when I headed to Flight Attendant Training in Minneapolis, Minnesota. Flying was a great opportunity, but I would have to leave my baby, again, and I was terrified. I convinced myself it was for us and we needed the change, so I jumped feet first into the opportunity. I was a different person in this phase of my life. I was the same determined woman that completed my

Alicia R. Stokes & Tyeisha L. Dalton

college degree with Iyana on my hip, but the quest for more was greater. I had to give Iyana more than I had when I was growing up.

It was freezing in Minnesota when I arrived for training. We were assigned a roommate and were required to study and pass assessments each week to keep our space at Flight Attendant Training. There was a melting pot of people there, all demographics and races. I immediately hit it off with Shannon, Brandon, and Nadkeya. We would study and push each other to succeed. The work each week would get harder and harder and my roommate eventually had to leave since she failed an exam. I remember her tears and the emotions; I was determined not to lose. I was not going home without a job.

Training was filled with drama. There were too many kinds of people for it not to be. The cattiness of the men and women there, I swear it was better than the Real Housewives franchise! There were lies, sex, same-sex encounters, and gossip!! My roommate at training was from Texas and she reminded me so much of Laurel, who was my roommate freshman year, and a wreck. She was catty and a race-baiter...basically, to her, black women were nothing special. In in some ways, it was empowering to me when she got sent home and I was excelling. She and I argued over dishes and politics and every day was certainly entertaining. I learned the power I had during that time, how that strength would intimidate people who would see in me what I couldn't. It taught me to stay to myself, to rely on my knowledge, and it reminded me that people are a product of their upbringing. Here I was fighting to make a better life for Iyana and many of the people here were too distracted to win.

When Dana, my roommate, packed to leave, Ms. Fiona became my roommate. It was a different energy and we pushed one another. She was older and married, had an amazing British accent, and she was super funny. We became fast friends. She would listen to me and support me and I would remind her that she was great and that we would finish this together, strong! One day, a few weeks before the final exam, Fiona was sent home for missing a few questions on the exam. I was sad, but I had a mission. She left me a note and what I remember of it, said: "Sweet pea, you are one of a kind" she told me to keep studying and get this job for my baby. I carried that reminder with me and I became a Flight Attendant.

Losing my Papa

I made it through training but not without darkness. See now, I was accustomed to the dark. So I learned how to walk in it. I experienced a great tragedy as I lost a vital piece of heart. I lost my Papa. He died while I was away at training. These lessons were coming at a price high in emotional pain, but I was determined to move forward. I had a choice to leave the training facility and return after the funeral. I remember the day my family notified the teachers. It was a day that started regularly, but I was homesick and missing my baby. I had a missed call from my mom. I planned to return the call during my break. I noticed the instructors whispering and looking in my direction and I became curious. It was time for a break, so I immediately went to call my mom. She was audibly upset but wouldn't tell me what was wrong. I learned later she had been asked not to mention my Papa. The instructors were supposed to inform me of the loss. I wondered about Iyana and the family because my mother was so worked up. The Instructor knocked on my door, so I ended the call and I thought I did something wrong. I panicked.

The worst pain ever cut through my body. I couldn't breathe. They got me some water and told me I had the choice to leave. I inquired about the steps needing action if I decided to go. I told them that I would think it over. I thought about it overnight and decided not to leave for the funeral. I would leave and be a week behind, missing the rest of the assessments, but I could return once the next hiring class got to the week I was currently in. I would graduate with people I didn't know and it would take longer to begin to make more money. No. That was the best decision because I needed to remember him as he was: full of love, soft gray hair, a laugh I loved that I don't hear anymore when I think of him, and so much love and support for me. I had learned to press through the adversity and I was tired of losing.

On the bright side, life was progressing and I was officially a "fly girl". I graduated, and life was headed in a positive direction. I held the title of Flight Attendant for just under a year or so when I was told I was being fired. I was devastated, I mean it was hard enough flying with minimal support for Iyana and the pay was not nearly enough. Still, I traveled places I never thought I would go like California, Arizona, North Dakota, and London. Before becoming a Flight Attendant, I had only been to Ohio and Missouri with my family, but now it was time to move on.

I was fortunate enough to make a quick transition into an Office Manager role for a chemical company through a temp agency. It was a great learning opportunity and I excelled running the office for ten-plus chemical sales associates. I transitioned from there to Volkswagen as an End of Lease Specialist, helping people end their vehicle leases. It was a better opportunity and increased my pay. I was not happy in my career during the time after college, but I was stable and working to take care of Iyana, so that was enough.

I was also full swing into planning a wedding as I was engaged Ian's dad by this time. I was so in love and my rose-colored glasses kept the sun out of my eyes, so I went on pretending life could not get any better. I can honestly say that the man I was with, during this time, loved Iyana as if she were his own child. He catered to her and loved her. He spoiled her and made sure all her needs were met. I thought it was the perfect relationship.

Baby Mama- Twice

In January of 2009, I discovered that I was carrying Ian, and I lived with that secret until I was showing. I was too embarrassed...unmarried and unhappy, again, but equally as determined to prove I would make it just like I did with Iyana.

I pressed forward with my Master's program at Walden, and I started school just weeks before learning I was pregnant. The Master's degree program I selected was in the business school. It was the Human Resource Management program at Walden University. I began this journey alongside my best friend and Iyana's godmother, Terika. President Barack Obama had a grant for single mothers to go back to school, so we decided our children, Kahmai and Iyana, should see us go all the way! Eight days after beginning my classes, my contract at work left me unemployed. I lost my job because I had a quota and I was not able to stay at my desk without getting sick. I was also at the doctor three times a week for non-stress testing. I was feeling all the sickness of pregnancy and still pushing through school.

Carrying Ian was not the most comfortable time. He was below the birth weight the entire pregnancy and I was sick all day long. It was a hard time for me as a woman. I watched my savings dwindle and there was not much support from Ian's dad in the areas that mattered. I went in for my weekly stress test and I noticed that the technician had an odd look on her face. She left abruptly to get the doctor. I looked at Ian's dad and I said to him "Something is wrong". The doctor walked in and gave me the decision to have a second cesarean voluntarily or I'd possibly end up there in an emergency. I decided to take the surgery and as I laid there having a challenging time, I could hear the beeping and felt the pressure of the operation. Finally, they removed my son and I was relieved. But I noticed that there was no sound. I did not hear crying. I looked up at his dad and he was frozen. He began screaming, "What's wrong with my son?" I was afraid, and I started crying and praying to God that we would hear something.

From behind the curtain laying on the table, I was helpless, numb. I cried and Ian's dad was asked to calm down by the hospital staff several times. He wiped my tears and was working to keep me calm when Ian cried out. It was a loud cry, but there was a moment where even that made me emotional. They rushed him to the NICU, the Neonatal Intensive Care Unit. It was then that I changed his name from Kodi Maxwell to Ian Xavier. It means "bright" and "the Lord is generous". It was perfect! Eventually, they released me to go home, and I had to visit my baby for a few weeks in the hospital.

I took the time to heal at home with Grandma for about five months and then I jumped right back into working part-time as a Banquet Server. It was easy to love the opportunity since I grew up in the same environment with my mother. I worked for Parties with Class, her old employer. She called the owner and he gave me an opportunity. I was willing to do whatever I had to do to take care of my children.

My relationship during this time was no walk in the park. I experienced so many things emotionally, physically and spiritually, so life had started to take its toll on me. For one, I had been staying with my grandma during the early months of Ian's life and she helped me a great deal. Ian's dad visited us and we often went to see his mother and family. It was a challenging time for me. I was in a relationship as a single mother of two, now. I am not sure that he kew that I felt any sort of way; like, I was alone in his absence, but I was becoming detached at the seams. After caring so well for another man's child (Iyana), he was not as active in his own son's life. I could not account for his time and whereabouts most days and we argued more often. I was able to get a full-time job working twelve-hour shifts, so between my babies, school, and sleeping, I was temporarily at peace.

My routine was standard. I woke up, got us all dressed, made breakfast, decided on dinner for the evening, and headed to work. Ian's dad would do school and daycare drop-offs and pick-ups, which took a load from me. After work, I went home to prepared dinner, bathe the kids, study and crash at the end of the day. I would get up the next day, on fumes, doing it all over again. I did not know this was preparing me, strengthening me for the times ahead.

One day I met Maria. She worked at Verizon Wireless, outside the mall. I was facing some management challenges at Underground Station, so I applied for Verizon to be a Sales Rep. I got a call-back thanks to Maria's referral and I killed the interview. I put my two weeks' notice at my job and started my journey at Verizon.

Lose to Win

What a difference a year makes. I started Verizon in November 2011 and by November 2012, I was excelling in my job and school and life was going well. I was focused and I was determined to finish my degree no matter what. No setbacks allowed and I did just that. However, when it was time for graduation, I could not go. I finished school in May of 2011, but Ian's dad did not support me at all. I was too proud to involve my family, especially since it required filling them in on all the drama in my relationship or ask for a handout, so I didn't attend my graduation. I never walked the stage and I wanted so badly to feel the emotion of the accomplishment in person, but I settled for having my degree mailed. I can honestly say that the only thing I regret in my life is not walking that stage and allowing my babies to see me in the cap and gown regalia of my Master's Degree.

By this time, the arguments between Ian's dad and me had gotten worse and ranged from his whereabouts to other women and even to my cooking, some days. I was always talking about him to my co-worker Philly, my good friend from Verizon. I'm sure that, some days, I drove her crazy! I remember she told me that one day when I had taken enough, all I could take, I would stop talking about him and end the relationship. Ian's dad and I were full-swing into a disagreement concerning the apartment and he left, angry. I had long stopped discussing my issues within our relationship with friends and now I was just going through the motions. Two days had gone by and we were not speaking. I decided on the morning of day three, since he had been staying at his mother's house, that if he came home and did not speak to me, I was done.

I got up and got us ready. The kids would be dropped off by me on this day. I had to start navigating solo and that day was a good day to start. Ian's dad returned, walked in and walked right by me without a word. And I was done. I grabbed the kids, left the house and called him telling him to be gone when I got off work. I cried most of the day and it impacted my job. I was mad at myself. I found peace in the decision, but I had to allow it to settle. When I got home, he was gone, and I went about the routine I had crafted in all the time I spent alone. I was broken. I had to choose me and I lost him, a man I surely loved more than myself. Yes, I loved him more than myself. I mean why else would I have taken so much from him? I felt like I was in love, but love was not in me and love was taking me out breath-by-breath and moment by moment. Five years in a relationship where I gave so much of myself that I had to find who I was again. It was painful and I was searching to feel whole again. I took some time to learn about myself and avoided dating like the plague.

I was so strong during this time, despite all the ways he still would discard me and leave me without assistance. He would promise to bring money and never come through. It was a hard time. I eventually had to get some support to make ends meet and moved to a place where I could cover the bills on my own.

It was during this time that I met Peyton's dad. And, honestly, I was not ready for a relationship. I tried and tried, but we ended up disagreeing and I walked away from him. I was so confused about all my " 'ships '" at this point in life. I couldn't even remember what all the fall-outs were about. But, if you add shame, broken relationships, abandonment, death, internally losing myself, and carrying pride, it describes the makeup of a broken and lost woman. It was a snapshot of my journey. I was lost, yet again, and I had to start working to find my way once more. I was not sure how, but I knew how *not* to. It was the best direction I could be in to win despite all that I'd lost.

Patchwork

I started going to therapy and it was good for me. The treatment revealed that I needed work on the inside. I had learned to mask the pain very well. I would smile big and bright on the outside, while on the inside, I was bleeding-out in desperate need of attention. I did not stay with it, though, and I believe I only prolonged my problems. While exiting therapy, my father had been trying to rebuild our relationship. Despite all the tools, I was just not interested. All he wanted, all he talked about, was being a better grandfather to my babies than he was a father to me. I shut him out as I felt that it was too little, too late for that.

Then one day, while at work, I got a call to rush to the hospital because my dad was not expected to live. I was devastated and I cried all the way to the hospital. I arrived and I saw that all of my family were there, together. I spent just under a week driving to and fro, working to tend to my daddy with my siblings and aunts. After a lot of prayers, God had turned his health around and he was discharged from the hospital. It was just not time for him to go yet. And, I felt that we had to support him.

We almost lost him, so I tried to make the best of the time with him after that. I loved my daddy's voice, but the next several days we spent togther, it was faint and he never talked loud anyway, so it was tough to hear sometimes. My family and I took turns sitting at dialysis with him. I found great joy during my time with him. I now wish that I had asked more questions or tried to learn more of who he was, but he often slept through it. I long to know his favorite color, favorite food, favorite song, anything to just talk to him and love on him, but that time has passed. I lost my daddy in March of 2012 and I felt shattered. I stayed quiet. No one could know the anger and hurt I was carrying inside. During this time I still chased him, but this time, he was not running. I was. Running to make the memories count and the moments last. To make matters more painful, I had another relationship go sour and I learned that Ian's dad had gotten married. This was only eight months after we split up.

The pain, the shame, and embarrassment I felt was immeasurable. I had endured what I believed was cheating, after all, looking at the short timeframe it took for him to marry. It was confirmation for me and I was angry. When I think about it, I had been cheated out of several firsts for my children and I sacrificed my needs for a long time. I was not even present for my son's first haircut because his dad allowed his cousin to take Ian to a barber one day, after daycare, while I was working. They sent me pictures and gave me a bag of his hair. I was just done, defeated, and depleted. I felt empty, as a mother, as I had missed concerts and first steps due to work. All of it in order to make ends meet.

In November 2012, I decided to go back to therapy. I had a terrible run-in at work with a customer that ended with me being rushed to the employee area after the woman got in my face and I didn't back down. I was a ticking time-bomb of emotions, waiting to explode at any moment. I would surely lose everything at the rate that I was going. I was in and out of relationships at this point, but I was determined to make the rules for my own life. If the men in my life would not follow them then they would be "released". I was determined to be in control and I was not letting it go ever again.

Shrink Me

Therapy saved me. Again. I had begun seeing a counselor, along with Peyton's dad, trying to salvage the on-/off-again relationship during an 'on' period. It had turned out to be something I needed for myself, so I decided to seek the healing I needed.

Therapy revealed that there was a little girl inside that required attention and I was determined to repair all that was broken. I learned in therapy how to cope with the past but not let it run my life, impacting my future. I had so many issues with abandonment and had grown accustomed to walking away from people, by myself, without blinking. Abandonment was second nature since it was all I knew. I ended relationships and never looked back. I would go 'cold' and not even flinch. Self-preservation was the name of the game for me.

We rarely consider the traumas of other people when we are going through life. We meet people or tend to our family with reckless words and behaviors with no real concern about the hurt they may have or the broken places the other person has been. Hurt people hurting people is real and I was angry, again. I was just seconds from breaking, snapping, and hurting someone. I was intolerable of people and their disrespect or disregard for my feelings. It was my way or no way and in maturity, I can honestly say I still struggle with this, but I am much better today. I am appreciative of my journey and I was able to face the darkness of my past. I was a hurt and lonely little girl on the inside, but the woman on the outside had learned to keep her hidden.

I was only kidding myself in my quest to tame that little girl. I began to write less and talk more. This helped me sort through communication issues and my feelings. I began to give and pray more. These things softened my heart and changed me so much. Most importantly, I worked on forgiveness. And even if the person I needed to forgive, my daddy, for instance, was gone, I had to do it for me. The path started in, seemingly, forgiving myself one day and one step at a time, a moment at a time. I had to purge, and the first thing was releasing the pain of my darkest hour.

Poem: The Darkest Night

Night has come, you lay helpless in the dark. Clothes on the floor from laboring a few days before. Stomach growling from hunger but no strength to cure it. You thirst after something more than water but refuse to move. You lie and say, "I am fine" in text messages and avoid calls. You yearn for more to your existence than unforgiveness and strife. Days become weeks, and darkness is all you see. There is no beauty in flowers, no love in your eyes, no passion in your stride, pride is welling inside. You refuse to be vulnerable enough to let anyone in. You were praying for better days and humility within. See, darkness has a way of blocking out the light. You try, and you try to see the beauty of life. In an instance you wonder what you have left to give.... is it worth the pain and grief that you hide and live? They say God has a purpose for your distress, but all you can feel is blood. Blood pouring from your heart and the wounds that people give. They give and give piercing your side your back your front.

Excruciating pain from your youth pours over your adult, and you no longer smile. It piles and piles up like a landfill of bones and forgotten things, trash, and rubbish. You consider your faith, thankful God is not like a man despite the enemy's plan. You lay in wait for the light to peek through the blinds. You are begging for light, even a glimmer of insight. The "Night" seems to last the tears flow forever, and you simply oblige. Praying, you hear a bird chirp, and the light creaks in. You exhale knowing, and you finally made it through the darkest night.... if only to make it through the darkest night!

Alicia R. Stokes & Tyeisha L. Dalton

    I wrote this poem as a release. Sometimes we live in secret with our darkness. I believe God has commissioned me to share my darkness as a testimony that not only brings relief to me but also helps someone else. Darkness is real. It is not to be taken lightly. People have taken their lives in this darkness. I pray for my sisters and brothers around the world living in this darkness. There are these places in our hearts that need healing. That broken little girl or boy inside needs healing. Seek help now, talk to a Therapist or Grief Counselor. The time is now to take your life back.

Chapter Four:

Release

My Darkest Hour

2006 **THROUGH 2012** was a tough time for me for several reasons. I experienced job loss, death of loved ones, failed relationships, and despite achieving the first Master's Degree in my family, I felt unaccomplished. The year 2007 took my Papa. In 2009, I was unemployed and pregnant with Ian. In 2011, I graduated with a Master of Science in Human Resource Management, but did not attend graduation and I ended my engagement. Then, in 2012, my heart was broken with the death of my father and I was falling apart at the seams. The recovery of heartbreak, the discovery of what I thought to be a new love interest, and a new career chapter were all positive things though, right? Well, as I began therapy, I realized I was haunted by a much bigger skeleton.

Thinking back to 2007, I was excited about life and the next steps since I was engaged to be married to Ian's dad and I was 22 years old. I was connected to this man with a ten-year age difference…*Those Damn Daddy Issues*, remember. I was in the final interview process for Northwest Airlines and things were 'looking up'. After all, I had endured a lot. I was grateful to see the sun.

I was working at Great Lakes Crossing mall at The Children's Place and I started feeling sick. All the pregnancy symptoms came crashing down on me at once and I began to panic. I was standing in a stall, the questions running through my head: Is he going to want this baby? Did I want this baby?

Alicia R. Stokes & Tyeisha L. Dalton

I was holding a positive pregnancy test. My co-worker was kind enough to bring with her to work and I was so sad. I was disappointed in myself. I allowed this to happen, again, but I had not done anything to change the process or the pattern, so why should I have a different outcome? I finished my shift, I went home, and I told him that I was pregnant. The look on his face was apparent. He was not happy, but not unhappy either. But there was not a drop of love in his eyes. He asked, "What you want to do"? In shock, I simply replied, "I will let you know". I prayed, I cried, and I prayed some more.

The next morning when I opened my email, I had been hired as a Flight Attendant. There was an offer and invitation to training. I decided that I could not have a baby right now and I convinced myself that it was my choice despite being one hundred per cent against abortion. Yet, I was terrified. We had been engaged for 6 months now and this man put the weight of the decision all on me. To me, it was a 'team' decision. I was not hurt enough to leave him alone but hurt sufficiently to question myself. I had been here before with Iyana's dad, but I walked away.

Life has a way of re-dealing lessons when you do not learn from them the first time. My first "real love" had told me to abort our baby and I refused. I did what I thought was standing up for myself in all the power that this newly found independence had afforded me. I stood up for myself and I had my baby. My choice, my way. I was six months into having someone raise her with me the way I imagined it should be like and, somehow, I expected a different outcome this time.

I was terrified as I booked the abortion appointment and conviction weighed on my heart, but I made it clear I was not paying a dime for the procedure and we would be going together. It was a beautiful office and the waiting room was full of women my age -and younger. We were there to get rid of what we deemed as a 'problem'. Looking back at that moment, I wish I could have talked to myself and those girls. The me I am today has a message of hope and love for myself and for those women, but I sat there in reality, lost and cold.

I remember talking to one woman who had a few children already and the baby made her spit like crazy. She said she was not having another kid. I tuned her out and I thought about my prayers. My prayers for God to direct me. And I questioned if those prayers had been answered through Northwest Airlines. I recall thinking that the email for a new job was not a Godly confirmation or approval to abort a baby. My baby. It was a better position that would allow me to see the world, so this time selfishly, I decided on an abortion. See last time I suppose I wrongly had a baby a man did not want, a decision I made of my own free-will because it is my body. Was that selfish? See, selfishness has a way of being funny;. There was no God in this decision, however.

The Process

The first step to abortion is a pill. I got the tablet in my cup, and I stared at it for a while. I asked him if he was sure, before I placed the pill in my mouth, and he said "Yes". He asked if I was sure and I am not sure if I even answered or just took the pill. I remember him saying shortly after, "I wonder if we should have kept it" and I was pissed! The nerve of him in that too-late moment to say this to me! I think I lost a piece of myself, again, in that moment.

I was wilting like a flower, dying in the middle of that room, feeling like he placed the burden on me by asking what I wanted to do. I remember feeling numb as they called my name. The pill started to make me feel odd in my tummy, like cramps. He kissed me and told me he would be waiting for me and it felt like the walk of death. I remember feeling cold as I entered the examination room and I shivered. I will never forget this day, the tools, the white coat that was bright as snow

Alicia R. Stokes & Tyeisha L. Dalton

the Doctor wore. Her face is a blur to me, as I replay laying down, but the Doctor was warm and pleasant and she seemed concerned about me. She appeared to be a kind woman and she told me the rules and the steps she would take, reminding me to relax. I remember a loud suction noise and light pain and, just as soon it began, it was over. I was emotionally done. I had an empty feeling and my heartfelt like I was dead. I felt lifeless.

I got dressed and was wheeled into a room to lay down for an hour and then I'd be released. There were other women there, each just as quiet as I was. Some sobbed uncontrollably in silence as I did. I asked God to help me, to help us. I must have dozed off from crying because I was awakened, gently and was escorted out. He was sitting there waiting, looking pitiful and I hated him. Literally hated him. For a moment in time, I hated his presence and existence and we walked to the car to head home.

We drove in silence, my back turned slightly away from him. We picked up my prescriptions and I decided I would keep my secret tucked away in shame. My child would've been thirteen years old this year. The irony of it all is that he wanted a girl and in dreams I have had, I believe that baby was a girl. I had had moments when I remembered I wanted a large family. Children, pets, white picket fence. You know, the works! I think of that baby often, a lot less now than I used to, but I recently had a full meltdown when I realized that the child was still a massive part of me. I was fasting and releasing and I actually grieved for that child and had to refocus for peace. I love my children and I love that baby just the same. I carry the pain, but God is forgiving. The trouble is genuinely forgiving yourself. I still have work to do, but I survived my darkest hour.

Poem: The Bitter Baby Mama

The tears continue building in my eyes, engulfed by anger, and I just see red. This is who I have become a ticking time bomb of emotions. I feel like I am busting at the seams trying to keep a face of integrity and a tough exterior. I'm hurting inside, and it is getting the best of me. Hatred fills me up, spilling over like a well during a storm, and I can't breathe. The past is suffocating me, and life is escaping me. The more I hold on to the pain of the past, and I lose more and more of me. There is no freedom living in the past. There is no peace living in the past. There is nothing left but useless memories of what will never be. I must release the hold the past has on me and cover myself to shield me from me. I feel the change; the scars serving as a reminder of where I have been. The present state of this storm is wreaking havoc on me, and I am losing control. Bitterness and disgust. I realize that I am slowly becoming a bitter baby mama. This cannot be. I just want to be free, free to be me... bitter free.

Chapter Five

More than just a B-A-B-Y M-A-M-A

THINKING BACK OVER THE trauma I faced as a child and entering motherhood, I never would have thought being a mother would affect me so much. I believe the title of baby mama is one that creates fear and uncertainty. This is not what I wanted for myself or any other woman raising a child alone. During the times I felt most alone, I had supportive friends. Many of whom lived the same misfortune of being labeled a "Baby Mama". We would support one another, talking for hours, and loving on the children. Our children are innocent.

The power Ian's dad had over me would eventually die down and I would 'rebuild' myself. The day I stopped mentioning him seemed vivid to me, but I was broken, tired, and unfamiliar with who I was anymore. Determined to move on since he had successfully diminished my vision of who I was. Yes, I blamed him for all of my issues. I set down my crown as I felt that I was damaged. It was easier not to self-reflect and not be accountable. Not to mention that he had remarried. I was a smoking gun and I was angry and it was all very unfortunate.

I had a friend in a similar situation, and she said to me, "Once it is over, prepare yourself now because you will watch him give someone else what he would never give you". I was living that. The devastation I felt was not because I was still in love with him, but because I was -yet again- left out to dry with questions, defeat, and broken promises.

Bitterness set in quickly as I replayed all the times I knew something was not right. All the times my intuition warned me, but I refused to stand up for myself. The hours lost in thought, the weight I lost from stress, the children I had to care for solely off of one income. It was all I could see. Months of lies, with no real help, was all I had. My heart was so black and blue. You could never tell from my smile, but I was dripping with pain. Two beautiful children and I felt ugly inside. The huge, downward spiral came from my belief that I was nothing more than a *baby mama*. Iyana's dad always reminded me of that with brash comments and rude remarks when I would not allow him his way. I was trapped in thought and space, leaving me with the belief that I was doomed. This was not how I pictured my life and I was so discouraged. My next few relationships were terrible since I could not break the emotional cycle. I could not recognize it. This reality was obtained too late. Much too late.

I had my fill of 'trash' and it was spilling over. I laugh, now, as I recall a running joke between my Grandma and an Aunt. It was not at all funny when it was presented to me as I found it offensive and it hurt very deeply. *Garbage picking*! That was the term my Grandma mentioned when she referred to my relationship choices. She told me "You got that degree and went garbage picking!" I moved from hurt into anger about the statement, but at this stage of life, I had found freedom in my past; promise, and strength in those lessons. And, I am no longer haunted by my mistakes. Now, I will not pretend this journey in what they call a 'baby mama' was meant to be easy anyway.

Marriage is said to be protected. You have two people raising a family. Except that, with divorce -along with other issues, you can still be reduced to a 'baby mama'. Instead, I think of the role in simple terms. I am a single mother and I am working to find positivity in doing it alone.

The strength of a woman is immeasurable. Women all over the world are facing adversities that require them to push through. I am no different. I continue to find restoration as I know that my children are watching my every move.

Alicia R. Stokes & Tyeisha L. Dalton

If I could tell my past-self anything it would be to know my *worth* and my *value*. The past is not meant to be lived in. It is to be used as a reflection. And, even though someone's history is prettier than mine, I am fully aware that the future is brighter because of what I have expereienced, where I have been and how God has carried me through it, all.

A Mothers Love

Not a lot of people know this about me, but one of the things I love most are exotic flowers. They are delicate and often times, a rare find. For me, there are similarities of this delicacy in being a mother. In thinking of my love for beautiful exotic flowers such as Bird of Paradise or the simple Calla Lily, I can see the similarities in -and my love for- my three children.

You see, the Calla Lily is easy to grow and they are neat and classy. By garden-flower description, they are perfect for gardening. The Bird-of-Paradise, however, are exotic flowers that resemble a crane, or bird, and make a lovely landscape plant. Just as these flowers differ, they both require love, proper tending, and water. These differences, to me, match my children.

Each child requires love and proper tending. They grow differently, learn differently; and, most of all, need individual love, differently. The love of a mother has subtle differences for each child and is always given to the one who needs it most, at the time. I refuse to believe there should ever be favorites. Each child requires you and your love. Just as each of them will recite memories of you, differently. I am careful of the memories I create for my children and they remind me of the beauty of their love, to embrace the moments.

As I danced around with Peyton this morning, listening to Deniece Williams' song, "Free", it brought to memory times like that with my mother. The brighter times. Often, these memories are not fond or positive at all so, this memory was twofold. I recall dancing around with Iyana and Ian, also, when they were babies, but I also recalled dancing with my mother, standing on my her feet, as a child. Or, as I got older, slow dancing with her in the kitchen while she cooked. There would be music blaring ranging from Marvin Gaye to Johnny Guitar Watson. Wow! It shows me that I do have positive memories and how I am learning to spend more time in those memories.

We spend so much time blocking out the good times because we are haunted by the ugly times. And, we hold on to them as such. This prevents forgiveness. It tightens the grip of anger and chastens our love for those we should forgive. Just as I cleared the positive, I felt the ugly, like a ton of bricks, haunted by her drug use and being second in her relationships; always feeling alone or outcast. I spent most of my life with this feeling and it is a daunting emotion that should've never had a place, to begin with.

Now, as an adult, I face the reality of this 'island' which I have created for myself where I do not allow people on any longer. Total isolation and pride are where I live and I am the keeper and protector of my heart and peace. Every time I had ever let someone in, I had been burned. Whether it was in relationships, friendships, co-parenting, and the likes. Things like this build character, but it also builds walls and resentment. Have you ever been there? I am not sure how to tear them down. I have been trying for a while now, the pressure has been building, but I have learned to stand firm to the promises of God and forgive. I hear that forgiveness is for *you*, not the person who hurt you. In all honesty, I had been lying to myself, trying to fool myself into believing I had forgiven Tyeisha. Times up! It is time to forgive and live truly!

Alicia R. Stokes & Tyeisha L. Dalton

The Glamorization of Single Parenting

Parenting can be challenging, especially when you have children, as opposed to just one child. As a single mother with children, there are layers added that you wish more people could understand. Having more than one child requires you to love each child equally, yet differently. You must respect each of their love languages and be sure no one ever feels slighted or as if there's a favorite.

Being a mother of two girls with a boy in the middle is especially challenging, at times, since there's something about the bond between a mother and a son that I never imagined. He still finds moments when he feels the girls get more attention or are luckier than he is. When I was grwoing up, there was nothing but boys for me to play with and be around. I was outnumbered and a tomboy.

I feel familiar with the emotions that Ian feels from time to time, even though the roles are reversed. He often questions what I'm able to do with the girls that we don't necessarily align to, so I find myself having to focus on more things that are driven and catering to him as well, like sports or a video game such as Minecraft.

Parenting has no manual, and unfortunately, even though you only get one chance to do it right, you simply do the best you can in the time you have to mold and teach them. What I find helpful is spending time with each of them, individually, teaching them as well as learning from them; and loving them in our own time together. I never understood the emptiness that my mother would have when she talked about her childhood while I was a child. I think that with a large family and the time that she was raised in, the challenge was showing love and affection and understanding the individuals that your children would become.

She tried to use her experiences to share with me. I just did not see it until now. She would always tell me, "You will understand when you are older". Sheesh, is that statement true! I finally understand her and how she raised me, giving what she could provide, which was the best she had.

I challenge myself to be a better parent than my mother and father were. I feel like doing it alone and not having the best space with their fathers is still a failure, however. I wanted to not only give them what I didn't have but surpassing that and pouring into them in ways that I wish had been done with me, catering to their self-esteem and self-worth; encouraging them and teaching them about counseling and doing their best. Teaching them to love one another despite what others tell me about having siblings being a rival or always a battle or fight, in addition to teaching them to care more about how they feel about themselves: seeing their worth, and forgetting the thoughts of others.

I did not grow up with my siblings, so I see those relationships differently and 'rosier'. I always imagined that having siblings would be fun and exciting and filled with love. The more I talk to my friends and people who have siblings, the more I understand that it this is not the case. It can be very combative and very challenging and now I find myself battling against that with my children as I "force" them to love one another and having them understand that *I* am the tie that links us together. Once my work here on Earth is done, I need them to be one-unit, a force that cannot be broken. I will keep pushing for my children to love one another and be kind to one another, to be different from whatever others tell them they must be to one another. All I can do is show the greatest examples that I can and know that those mistakes I may make are okay. Communicating and talking to your children is the best thing that you can do, especially in this age of technology.

Alicia R. Stokes & Tyeisha L. Dalton

We ought to be mindful of what our babies are consuming and what we allow them to see *us* consume. Historically, in the African-American community, we operate under the "do as I say, not as I do" mentality. In my experience, this is not conducive to raising children because they are much smarter and compelled by us.More than we may know. Despite trying to have conversations in private or hide things from them, they are always listening.

I am comfortable in my skin, today, and the decisions I make are made more confidently. I will not pretend I'm not haunted by those things in my closet anymore, but I refuse to let that determine who I am or who I'm going to be. The past is the past and cannot be erased. All I can do is move forward, accept God's grace is sufficient, and show my children I am worthy of being their example. There is no real glamour to single-parenting. It requires sacrifice. And, sometimes, you get dirty!

Is it Enough?

When I think about parenting and I think about the sacrifice, I find myself wondering if the sacrifices are ever enough. We love our children so freely, openly, and unconditionally and it is returned tenfold as they love us beyond comprehension. Probably more than even the love that we feel from our own parents. As I reflect on my childhood, I find myself in a battle with myself, continually trying to ensure that I am raising whole, functional people whom are not produced in chaos, negativity, and fear. As I think about those who have lost parents such as I have, without a connection or relationship, I feel empty. I find myself battling against the demons of what could have been, what wasn't, and what should have been. I often wonder if, as parents, you know to do more than what you have before you. You can only do what you know to do and the rest is a mystery.

GRACEFULLY BROKEN: A JOURNEY OF SELF-DISCOVERY

Eeach day is a chance to start over and do something better or different. There is no manual and there is no script. There is nothing written in the sand that teaches you how to parent. Every day is an opportunity to give life to a person that the Lord has blessed you with and to cultivate them to be functional human beings, as you share with them love and lessons along the way.

This journey that I began 13 years ago, being a mother, I had no idea what I was in for. I had no idea the amount of love that would be produced from the child the Lord blessed me with. I had no idea how much heartache and anguish and blood, sweat, and tears would be utilized to raise her, to raise them. Here I stand 13 years later, a mother of three equally as baffled by what each day presents as a mother. Living in the moment, embracing and capturing memories.

My one hope is that when I am called home, I have left enough memories ingrained in them that, at each turn, each thought, each decision, and each waking moment they remember me and never lose sight of the love that I have for them.

There's something so great about parenting. In the sacrifices, you begin to feel alive. But, if you are not careful you can lose yourself. And, amidst learning and growing and knowing who you are, as an individual and being someone's parent, there is a great joy. As I reflect on where I have been and where I am now, I find myself emotionally driven to be better for them. After all, they are the most exceptional works of art I have presented to the world.

The nine months that you carry a child, you never know exactly who you have birthed and will bring into the world. You consider the likes of President Barack Obama, Miss Maya Angelou, and think about how sacrificial you have to be. You wonder if you have the tools to produce the greatest additions the world has ever seen.

Alicia R. Stokes & Tyeisha L. Dalton

Gaining control of my life, carefully and strategically avoiding mistakes, so that I do not keep falling. Attacking my dreams with vigor and passion. Not losing sight or focus and aspiring to have and be more than before. A new day. Fresh anointing with each passing hour. God's plans are always certain. The objective is navigating through life operating in his will. The past is just that, living there is a choice but learning from it is the goal. Teaching my children this is essencial to breaking the cycle.

The more you imagine where you want to be, you cannot help but consider where you have been. It can be very distracting. You cannot get past what has been lost. You have won so many battles pushing through the storms that have come and gone. Many alone and in silence and some loud and in public. The Lord has been present through it all, of this I am sure. Without Him you would have surely fallen, committed suicide, aborted dreams, given up, and the enemy would have won. The time is *now* to push through the current storm. The enemy knows you are close, so he attacks your mind. He wants you to use your body, your self-esteem, your worth, and value to acquire the love mom and dad never gave.

People may never understand the places you have been. They are not supposed to. The ugly part of the path you have traveled is troubling and it haunts you. You wonder if the pain could have been avoided and could you have been spared some of the pain? You wonder how you have come this far. Then you remember that the 'tests' and 'trials' produce testimony. And that produces healing. I believe when you finish reading this book and learn about my journey, our journey, you will be blessed and understand life.

The mission is about pressing forward. It will have potholes, rocks in the roads, and even broken glass. There will also be smooth paths and light to get through the darkest hours if we keep God with us. This life is a journey so Live This Unscripted Journey!

Even though I had always wanted children when I was young and I wanted to give them what I missed out on, I never imagined repeating the cycle of single parenting. I imagined a large family with four children and a puppy. A family full of love, stability, and both parents working together. I never had this example. I just rationalized that is how it would be, had to be, must be. Life showed me my plans were not impossible but my plans were not going to happen the way I thought. And my ideas? Well, my ideas, my thoughts about relationships could be cloudy. At 21, I was a single mom and a college senior with no husband or plan for marriage in sight.

I was devastated and I felt defeated, but I had my determination to complete my degree, seeing there were many who said that I would "ruin my life". All while I was pregnant, I ran into people -from past administrators to old friends and even family. They did not think I would be unwed and pregnant or irresponsible enough to get knocked up before I experienced life. They made me question me, doubt me, feel deflated, and wondering what life had for me. People will do that to you. They will break your stride with hurtful words. They project their fears and their dreams onto you, and when you fail you fail them, too. It is such a heavy burden for a frightened child that just had a child of her own. They say 18 makes you legally an adult and I think that is an awful pressure for our youth to endure. I was nowhere close to being ready to "adult" the way I had to when I had Iyana. My twenty-first birthday was filled with breast pumps, burping cloths, and diapers. While my friends were celebrating their first legal drink, I was battling nursing my week-old baby.

I realize I made choices that pushed me full-throttle into motherhood, adulthood. Had I even lived? Did I know what I was also doing? Would I be able to love her and provide for her? I was determined not to fail myself, and now I had to work harder not to abandon her too. More pressure, right? There was a full schedule for the rest of that year. I had Iyana with nine months left of my senior year. I woke up, pumped her

Alicia R. Stokes & Tyeisha L. Dalton

milk for the day, loaded the car, dropped her at daycare, and then for a few hours, I was just a college student, and it was such a relief.

Poem: Life has no guarantee

Life has no guarantee or promises, it isn't fair or always pretty
It has crooks and turns and pebbles in the road
It brings along trial and tribulation
It brings sunshine and love
Life has no guarantee
It pours out unreasonable portions at times
It forces you to fight battles you would retreat from
It requires you to be vulnerable when you want to be tough
It decides the weather and destination of the wind
Life has no guarantee, and it is a blessing each day to get the experience again
It is a blessing each day you open your eyes and live
It is a blessing each day you have functioning senses and limbs
It is a mystery this thing called life there is no secret to its mastery
You just get up and live… Life has no guarantee

Chapter Six

Diamonds

I LEARNED ABOUT THE formation of natural diamonds early. I took to their beauty and I fell in love. I also have a passion for rare gems. I love their beauty and imperfections. Diamonds, in their natural state, require very high temperatures and pressure to produce the loook of what we know as diamonds. Natural diamonds, unlike man-made diamonds, have internal flaws that occurred during the stones' formation and those flaws are tell-tale signs of the pressure the rock endured. In this phase of life, as I look at my body and examine my thoughts and memories, I recall the pressure.

In the new chapter of my life where I am comfortable and confident in who I am, those flaws are an accessory. I recognize the storms I have been through in the last twenty-plus years of my life and I was working overtime to eliminate the very pressures that were producing victories and purpose in my life. . Constraints such as what others thought, fear, lack of faith, darkness, and single-motherhood all plagued me at once.

In the 35 years I have been alive I have traveled, gained knowledge through education and personal experiences, and I have heard discouraging words. I have had more pain than I think one person should endure, but I am still standing. If I were to be honest with myself, I have accomplished milestones in life that defy the odds of my community like a first-generation college student and surviving living with a parent with an addiction.

I do recognize that God has 'kept' me when events have gone smoothly. I never was truly alone or without the necessities of life such as food, clothing and shelter. He does the same for me today as my children age, as I plan for retirement, marriage, and longevity. I have hope and recognize everything we go through is purpose-filled. And, no matter the detour, the journey is set to finish the same way...God-planned!

Love- Loving Others Vs. Loving Ourselves

Love is something that grows from within and spreads outward. There's something so great about understanding the manifestation of self-love. People go to great lengths for love, not fully understanding that the love they are requesting is already within them. A person on the outside can only add/contribute to that love. If you are seeking love and you fail to understand the importance of self-esteem and self-love, you are doing yourself a great injustice. Often, we grow old and we have ideas that were passed down to us generationally. Many of these 'ideas' should not have ever been introduced to us. For example, in our families, particularly black families, we tend to pass down generational phrases, superstitions, and even ideas that water-down any promise of the future. There comes a time when we must stand guard and heal. This healing must be done on your own as healing is the most important thing that never gets appropriately passed down, generationally.

How does one heal from brokenness? How do we recover from the guilt of the past? When do we stop tearing off scabs on wounds that should be healed, creating a fresh wound? Love and hatred often begin within us, as we start to analyze every piece of our being from our hair at the top of our head down to the soles of our feet. We become focused on who others think we should be and we never consider who WE are or who we are "meant to be". The people who matter the most will uplift us and when they identify a weakness in us, they will

Alicia R. Stokes & Tyeisha L. Dalton

help us grow. They will not use the information to tear us down. As I work to teach my daughter at the ripe age of 14 about her beauty and understanding, it isn't defined by the boy who thinks her butt is big but more about who she has determined she is.

As a mother, I want to shield her and protect her from everything, so the challenge is teaching her but allowing her to experience things on her own. Allowing my children to experience life. The last thing any parent wants is a child that doesn't love themselves, but the one thing I'm learning is that self-love is taught. How do you pour into your child what you are lacking? Well, the answer is simple: you must observe your weaknesses and take inventory. Once you can sort through your mess, you can engage your child, boosting their image of image of themselves and, along the way, their image of you.

I find myself being extremely careful about how I display myself before them. I remember dating someone, once, and my daughter asked me if I was desperate because of the way I allowed myself to be treated or spoken to, in addition what I accepted for myself. I had to beat her to these questions. I need to self-analyze and ask myself if this were my daughter how I would respond or behave. A quest for knowledge when you have children is a little bit different because they are impressionable and even when you think they are not looking, they are. When you feel they are not listening, they're in tune to you. I hope that she sees the beauty in the mess that I am. And, as I work to shape her and remove generational curses, I hope that she understands that I do it out of love.

Learning to Love Again

The Bible tells us in 1 Corinthians 13:4-8 "Love is patient, love is kind. It does not envy, it does not boast, it is not proud. It does not dishonor others, it is not self-seeking, it is not easily angered, it keeps no record of wrongs. Love does not delight in evil but rejoices with the truth. It always protects, always trusts, always hopes, always perseveres. Love never fails." NIV

One of the things I consider myself to be, is a lover. I know what I want and need in a relationship. Some things are *respect* and *financial security*. What I know, in my experience, is that love is not enough. A relationship can have love and two people can love one another and still crash and burn because love is a verb. It is an action word. It requires work to be sustained and I had to learn to love. Not only as I want to be loved, but also, Biblically; and to the standard of the person you are with, as well as mine, own. Love languages are real. And this can, also, be where the action comes in. Learning to listen and care for one another in love is an action. At times, it has to do with just being present, when you are needed.

Marriages that last fifty years have a foundation of action. It's two people who wake up every day and decide to navigate life together through a connection they share. They flourish in change and accept that every day takes work to have longevity. It's not smiles and roses every day, but a focus. It is to "stay above the belt" with disagreements and comments towards one another. Communication is essential as a foundation, learning to speak from the heart, openly and wisely. Relationships are valuable lessons.

Closing

Writing this memoir has been both tumultuous and empowering. It forced me to call to memory many moments in my life when I never thought I would make it through. Times in my life where I felt like giving up, even though I have had several wins. The losses have been plentiful, but I am proud of my accomplishments and the levels of greatness I have reached. And, that this book is completed.

The journey of this book started as an idea to inspire single mothers who have been through the fire from the perspective of a woman never married, a divorced woman, and a woman in a marriage caring for her children. The original idea didn't come to fruition, but Alicia and I forged a friendship that I would not trade for anything in the world, as we poured out on these pages. I am blessed to share in this journey with her and I hope and pray that your life can be shifted in as positive a way as mine has been, with God at the forefront. I am living and loving through His saving grace. Until next time!

Afterword

Tyeisha has been a part of my life since 1998. We met in the halls of Murray Wright High School in Detroit. She was friends with my boyfriend's sister. We shared a cordial hello, in the hallways but nothing more. I noticed she was always smiling and seemed happy. Her smile was so infectious! I always saw Tyeisha as one of the "Cool Kids" and I, a nerd. I was somewhat quiet during my first two years at Murray Wright with few friends. Tyeisha had many friends and belonged to various school clubs giving the opportunity to be around our peers. In eleventh grade, Tyeisha and I began to have more classes together, thinking back most of our college-prep classes were also. Our friendship grew stronger to where we wanted to spend time together outside of school, growing into a circle of friends. We were known as "The Fellas", primarily because there were more guys than girls in the group. I feel college set the actual trajectory of our "sister-ship". We have had our fair share of heartfelt talks, from boyfriend's to family issues, disagreements over liking the same boy and feeling isolated. We enjoyed college parties, concerts, and celebrating life achievements: our children's births and obtaining goals. Through it all, we continue to allow ourselves to trust each other with our heart's secrets and remain vulnerable. She is genuinely one of the few people I can talk to without reservation or judgment. I never knew how much pain was hidden beneath her smile. As we grow older, I am amazed by the depth of her story.

Tyeisha is an inspiration, as a good friend should be. If you are fortunate enough to have good friends, you will find that you have a personal cheering section and hardest critics, but it's all out of love. In life, there are always challenges, and they become easier to endure when God blesses you with a true, genuine friend. Tyeisha is just that!! By being open and exposing her vulnerability to the world to read, she is allowing us to grow with her. That is an accurate representation of

Alicia R. Stokes & Tyeisha L. Dalton

God's love shining through her. She could have easily allowed herself to be consumed with frustration, resentment, and anger, but instead, she exhibits strength, positive disposition, and love no matter what obstacle comes her way. She continues to keep God as her focal point. Reading her truth allows people, mainly other women, in similar situations, to have a glimmer of hope. Her experiences are truly inspiring and motivational. Tyeisha's path of finding herself may not have been easy, but nothing worth having ever is. Realizing nothing can get in the way of God's purpose in your life is powerful! Enjoy the read.

~ Jasmine Booker

Poem: Turbulent Reflections

Memories are a beautiful symphony harmoniously living in the mind's eye.

Flooding, swimming through the waters against the current.

Turbulent reflections. Darkness.

Light.

An array of visions.

A prism of green and orange hues.

The present forces you to perch on the branches of the past and reflect...

Turbulent Memories

To bring this full circle, we present testimonies submitted by our friends, family, and others, offering insight into this journey of discovery and learning. Hopefully, these stories will empower you and help you overcome!

Alicia R. Stokes & Tyeisha L. Dalton

Testimonials

From the Streets to Victory

I would like to give thanks to God, who is the head of my life. I made it through the storm and survived!

I was on drugs for many years, but in the last four years, the Lord has kept me strong. It was a struggle for me. I stopped and started repeatedly. You just get tired of being tired, I had to stop before I killed someone, or someone killed me. I was hurting myself; I was burning on the inside, and my family suffered greatly. There were times I wanted to end my life many times. I had the tools to quit, support from family, and resources at my disposal even that did not seem to be enough. I just had to quit. Drug addiction is funny like that, and I had so many triggers that would send me back into the drug life when I would stop. So, everything had to change. I started going to church, staying home more, surrounding myself with my daughter and grandchildren doing things with them, and spending all my money. This way, I would not have any to spend on that drug. I had to stay away from wet faces and places as they say and believe me, and it was very hard. Realizing I had no friends, I prayed every second, minute, and hour of the day. God started to place people in my life who were not on drugs because all I knew was druggie friends, and they really were not friends.

I was lost for a while, a long while. I even went to prison. I have a lot of chapters in my life, all of which, I could go on and on. I want to write a book about my life, and I'm sure it would be a best-seller. So much of what I have seen and experienced, sharing with those who struggle with addiction today, that there is a better way of living, and you too can overcome triumphantly and victoriously. Drugs are indeed a dead end. I lost so many people along the way, and through sharing my trials and tribulations, I hope to be a vessel to help save someone else. Once addiction leaves, you become unsure of yourself and steals everything from you. Losing your self-worth, family, respect, and leaving you feeling worthless and feelings of depression. Everything is unsettled in the pit of your gut; from who you were in the past and restlessness sets in, however, you can start healing. Trust and believe some people will begin to treat you differently but forget them. Those people will try and keep you bound to your past, but don't let them. They will even use it against you when they get a chance, and if you are not careful, you will be right back out there. So please, take my advice and stay away from people who are not encouraging you and pushing you to keep on the right path. I have so many testimonies, and I could go on and on, but I hope this will help someone with their recovery. My walk was not an easy one, and if you have never been there, you can't tell my story. Not until you have walked in my shoes. No one can explain it better than my God and me. I will always ask God why me. I stay prayed up when it comes to haunt me, and I ask God to regulate my mind, body, and soul. If you have an I want to quit attitude, I made it, and I know if I did anybody can. I made it through the storm, and I would like to apologize to my daughter, grandchildren, mother, my father, rest his soul, my family, and, most importantly, myself. Thank you, Father God, I made it through the storm. I Surrender My All, and one day I will share my story!

~ **Christine Dalton**

Alicia R. Stokes & Tyeisha L. Dalton

Self-Love

Today, I cried not due to sadness, but extreme happiness, and I am forever thankful. See, it has not always been this way, and I used to live in a dark world. I felt like a dark cloud was still following me, and I held belief and continual thought that God put me on this earth just to fail miserably at everything. The oldest of four, raised in a single-parent household, with the absence of my biological father. I was raised by my sisters' father. It was while in the fifth grade, I learned my sister and I didn't share the same father, which resulted in me hating myself thinking my own father did not want me. I thought he didn't love me. At the age of 14, I had to give up my childhood, to work to help my mother with the bills. I was taught early on that my feelings or putting myself first was never an option.

Six months after my 21st birthday, I had my first real relationship. A month into the relationship, I became pregnant. I was both excited and nervous. I grew up in a household where we never said I love you or even hugged one another. This is something I knew for sure I wanted to change with my daughter. My relationship with her father was crazy from the beginning. I was the girl who never really had female friends. I always had male friends. He instantly didn't like that, so I cut off my friends. The crazy thing is he had female friends, and if you dare to say anything, it was World War III. It was rarely physical abuse; it was always verbal and mental abuse. He had to party every weekend. I would come home drunk, and I had to play nurse. He would tell me my family did not love me, only he loved me, and I believed him. I could not enjoy myself when I went out, we would argue, or he would call every five minutes. I was told numerous times how I wasn't pretty and that nobody would want me, and if they did, it would only be for sex. We had our second child seven years after our daughter, and I know you are thinking, how did I stay with him another seven years? I sacrificed my happiness for my daughter's happiness. I felt her life would be so much better if both parents were in the same household. Growing up having both parents in the home was what I always wanted.

My second pregnancy was hell, he was cheating, and he didn't even want me to keep my baby. I used to walk two miles to a bus stop every morning because he was out with the car. The depression started, I hated my life, and I cried so much. I told myself he would change, just stay. After giving birth to my son, things got worse. I started doing everything literally on my own, cooking, cleaning, working, and taking care of the kids. I cried every night for a year straight, just asking God why me? If you love me, why put me in this situation. In December 2015, my biological father passed away. When I had my daughter in 2007, his first grandchild, he came back into our lives, and things had been right. I remember calling and telling my kids dad that my dad was gone. He celebrated his birthday the night before, so when I called, he was still drunk. I shared the news, and he said okay, he would call me back. Later in the day, he sent a text saying how sorry he was to hear what happened, and he would pray for me.

I took his passing very hard, but I tried to stay strong for my daughter. I didn't realize it, but she was trying to stay strong for me. During the whole ordeal picking out caskets and just preparing not to see my father again, my kids' father was never there. This was my breaking point; everybody who he said did not love me was there in some way. It was clear at that time who loved me and who did not. One day I had a conversation with my Aunt Gwen, we never really went into detail about my relationship, but she knew I was unhappy. She asked me what I wanted out of life. I started telling her what I wanted for my kids, that I wanted them to be happy to go to college and have a different experience than me. I will never forget what she said, she said "no, what do you want for yourself?" and I paused, I did not know. Nobody ever asked me about myself, so why would I think of myself when I had kids to worry about. My aunt asked me what I want for myself still replayed in my head; I ended my relationship with the kid's dad maybe a year later. It was the best decision I ever made but one of the hardest. I started going to church and praying more, but I was ready to change for the better.

I still am not where I would like to be, but I am mentally in a better place with myself. I love myself, and if you were to ask me today what I want for myself, I would like to smile more and to really experience love. I would also love to get my degree, travel just experience life itself. My favorite theory is that broken crayons still color. I allowed people to break me down just because they were broken. Yes, I'm broken, and I am not ashamed to admit it, but my life story has not ended, it's just getting started. I am overly excited about my life, for living. I never in a million years would have thought the girl who wanted to kill herself would be so happy to live. This year I laughed more than I cried, my confidence is through the roof, I used to get so nervous talking in front of people now you cannot shut me up. I take more selfies, I am happy!!!

~ **Stephanie Brown**

Healing: Finding Love

I am one of those women who have found love after abuse. I was married to a physically and mentally abusive man for five years. I was choked and beaten simply because he was a narcissistic sociopath. In May of 2001, I incorporated my "safety net" and left my husband, three children in tow, and I made it out by the skin of my teeth!

From 2001-2003 while going through my divorce, I prayed incessantly, reading books and blogs. I read everything I could to learn about domestic violence as I knew I wanted to one day be in a healthy relationship and not stay trapped in the "cycle." Fast forward to 2018, and I have had my fair share of dating. My experiences shaped me into a stronger woman. I knew what I wanted and didn't want. My tolerance for BS was and still is ZERO! I took off three and a half years and sat still. I decided. No men and no sex, and I gained CLARITY! At the end of 2018, I met my now-husband, and through this relationship, I have learned what a real man is, a real man treats you with complete respect. He is caring, gentle, and kind. A real man loves you for who you are, your likes, and your dislikes, goals, and ideas. I have a husband that I never thought existed. My marriage is beautiful, and it's free of abuse and fear. Our house is a happy place, filled with love. I'm a blissful bride, and I'm so thankful I can say I have found love after abuse. My key to finding love was allowing myself to heal, to grieve, and to learn to love myself.

~ Denise Arnold

Alicia R. Stokes & Tyeisha L. Dalton
My Myracle

I was always a fixer, an unmovable force when I set my mind to something! I did not know that a strong will, the strength everyone admired so much, would soon be put to the test. It has been said, and you never know how strong you are until you must be. I have always been considered a strong one, whether it be family or friends.

At the age of 27, I was diagnosed with SLE (commonly called Lupus) I thought my most significant obstacle in life would be living with an incurable autoimmune disease. I did all the reading and lifestyle changes, and I told myself, "I got this!" In the first year, it was rough, to say the least, I experienced chronic joint and muscle pain, even hair loss, and then I started experiencing numbness in my fingers and toes. Further testing determined I had Raynaud's disease, a disorder that restricts blood flow to certain areas of the body. Bouts of pneumonia would reveal a rare lung infection called BOOP, and fluid on my heart. It took almost a year before I was given a diagnosis, and at times, I thought I was going to die because I did not know what was going on with my body. I felt like the control and resolve I used to model so effortlessly was slowly being etched away. At times all I could do is press forward for my daughter, MaKenzie. She is so full of life and energy, so I refused to let these illnesses affect her too.

Once I was given each diagnosis, I did the work to manage my symptoms, and to be honest, just knowing what was wrong with me, my mind was more at ease because I could face it head-on. At the age of 33, after passing out at work, I was diagnosed with Pulmonary Arterial Hypertension, another incurable disease. I was told the pressures in my lungs could cause heart failure. At this point, my doctors advised me to be cautious in deciding to have more children because of the possible terminal risks that could come along with pregnancy, labor, delivery, and postpartum care. If I became pregnant, there was only a 40% chance I would survive. I have always wanted to have another child, but I also understood MaKenzie needed me, and whatever the future held, I would not risk it for a dream, a miracle. One of the hardest discussions I had was to tell the man I loved at the time I could not give him children. I felt like I lost a part of me. But, in October 2018, I found out I was pregnant. Now, I was truly faced with the most significant obstacle of my life, choosing my life or the life of my unborn child. I was about to turn 35, and I already had a beautiful ten-year-old daughter, was it worth risking my life not to see her grow up? But I felt something I had not felt in a while. I felt an assurance, determination, and honestly, excited than I had in a while about the future. I decided to go through with the pregnancy.

Several people, some very close to my heart, told me I was crazy and selfish for taking this risk. I reminded myself that God would not put more on me than I could handle, and I know myself and my capabilities better than anyone. I did not let the negative comments change what I always wanted or my thoughts on what was meant to be. For the first seven weeks, I saw doctor after doctor with each one saying, "We cannot handle this type of high-risk pregnancy. You may want to consider a medical termination." I turned to those closest to me, and they reminded me if it's meant for me to have this baby, God would make away. At 11 weeks, a high-risk OB sat me down and asked, "Are you 100% committed to this pregnancy? And do you have a support system around you?" I answered bitterly, "yes", thinking he would be another pessimist. Surprisingly he said, "We can't handle this type of pregnancy, but I know people that can." With one phone call, he transferred my care to the University of Michigan's medical team. Having knowledge of what the two diseases could do to my body under normal circumstances, I began strategically removing all stress from my life, even if that meant not talking to or dealing with certain people during the pregnancy. Then I followed all of the doctor's orders, but most of all, I put my faith in God, and I prayed every day for a healthy me and a healthy baby. I went to church every Sunday, and I leaned on my support system daily for those reminders that "I got this," and I remained positive. I found myself in a place in my life where I forbid anything stealing my joy.

At 34 weeks (6 weeks early), my baby girl decided to grace the world with her presence. Even though she was considered premature, there were no complications. I got my "Myracle"! I brought home a healthy four-pound baby girl all because I put my life and the life of my children in God's hands. Everything I have endured over these past eight years was not meant to break me but to show me where my real strength comes from.

~ Shari Ivery

Life After Death

Life truly is a box of chocolates, and you never know what you are going to get. As women, we can portray, we have it all together, but be immensely broken battling the thing we hate facing, which is ourselves and reality. My hardest battle was the demise of my marriage, but as I reflect, it was the fact I had failed at something I gave my all. We all hate failure, right? This was a battle I never wanted to face because it equated to death. Death hurts and is nothing to celebrate. Always remember God makes no mistakes, and when he said he would never leave or forsake you, that is real. In the end, I found love for myself, and death is just a cleansing to restore you back to the Beautiful, Bold, Empowered Woman God created us to be. There are Tokens I picked up along the way. Tokens = Words of Affirmation! The two affirmations that I spoke while battling death were "I am happy," and "I am expecting GREAT news." These words have changed my life chile! I stand on the scripture, "For she is clothed with strength and dignity and laughs without fear of the future" Proverbs 31:25 ESV. I am "Doing The Most" with no regrets, and you should too! Do the work hunni!

~ Kimberly Norris

Alicia R. Stokes & Tyeisha L. Dalton
College Ain't For Me

I met the love of my life, and I knew from that moment that I wanted to get married and have children. In high school, I knew or believed college wasn't for me. I didn't find school exciting, and my grades were average. I attended an HBCU; however, I still lacked inspiration and motivation. So that's what I did. I got married and began to have children. Fast-forwarding life began to change just as life is beginning for me; I got married, gave birth to a child, and moved into our first apartment. As it began it ended, instead of me being a wife with two children, I became a single mom.

Being a single mother was not something I asked for or imagined; however, it was very traumatic. My status of single parenting propelled my motivation for continuing life and working hard to provide for my children without the support of any kind from my ex-husband. I knew something was missing, but I couldn't place my finger on it, but God opened doors to jobs that would allow me to provide for my family. During this trying time, the Lord showed me how to manage my money. I believe I was led to enroll in community college. As a single-parent and the difficulty of finding a sitter for my children, I was only able to take one class per semester. Some semesters didn't allow for enrollment every semester. In August 2011, I obtained my associate's degree from Macomb Community College.

As the world continues to change, the internet became a "big thing," and God provided yet another opportunity to attend school at Rochester College. This was all done online in an accelerated program. I, with the help of the Lord, finished my bachelor's degree in April of 2017. For someone narrow-minded, I did not believe let alone think I was college material. Accepting the idea, college didn't matter, I not only obtained one but two degrees. I learned a college education did matter; it built my self-confidence and self-awareness. Today, when I look over my life and think things over, I see God's hand all over it. God used me to show my children that you can do all things through Christ Jesus. So, instead of passing on to my children's fear and lack of confidence, I believe God built me up so they could learn to soar at life with HIM. My children witnessed my example, both graduated from high school and immediately went to college. I am eternally grateful to God for the sacrifices he required of me.

~ **Cecelia Wilson**

Alicia R. Stokes & Tyeisha L. Dalton

Advice

Wisdom Doesn't Come Without Pain

It would indeed be a disservice if our stories didn't at least spark an emotion within you. A feeling that puts your heart at ease as you vividly recall a time when you wish you knew then what you know now. While writing our stories collectively, we reached out to women and men from all walks of life to talk about their stories; their hurt, insecurities, and mishaps left unaddressed as little children. Having encountered some costly lessons, we owe it to our daughters and sons to share our stories in hopes that generational curses will be broken.

"I wish I didn't put my all into a man without working on myself, it's ok to support your man and be his backbone, but don't forget about yourself."

As women, we are natural caretakers and nurturers. It's just this innate ability we have even as young children to tend to things we love. I watch my daughter, who is five years old, play with her baby dolls, and take great care of them. She often tells me how she's going to make a great mother and wife. I marvel in her tenacity, yet I'm concerned she'll lose her identity in being a mother and wife even worse not know who she is, to begin with. I find so many women, myself included, become of dating age and immediately go into mother and wife mode before we even have the slightest idea of who we are. Most of us deal with brokenness and challenges from our childhood and are so desperately looking for love in the wrong places. To prove our love, prove our worth, confirm we are "ride or die," we put our all into our men to earn some badge of honor for our loyalty, dedication, and commitment. Unfortunately, most of the time, we are depleting ourselves and pouring from an empty cup trying to help our men see who "they are" before we even know who "we are." It's not our job to help a man become a man, and it's his parents! Besides, we have no idea what it even takes to be a man we are women. God's design for us in relationship/marriage is explicitly to be a helpmate to our man, not his secondary mother. We simply cannot raise a man! If you find yourself in a situation like this, I strongly advise you to reevaluate your relationship. Giving of ourselves entirely with no reciprocity is a for sure a recipe for disaster with an extra serving of resentment. You'll find yourself depleted and angry, wondering why what you do and what you so freely give never seems to be good enough. The men we are so freely depleting ourselves for just might move on after we've finished "raising" them. After all, that's what they are supposed to do, right? The sad thing is they don't owe you a dang thing! Do yourself a favor and get to know who you are, fall in love with yourself, and get to know what God says about you. All the other things a good man included will be added to you. Focus on his word and his word alone!

~ *Alicia*

"I wish I knew being alone is better than being in an unhealthy situation."

There is so much to be learned in alone time. In alone time you learn to love yourself, to focus on the things you genuinely need, and you discover who you are all over again. When we grow up and head out into the world, we believe and are so sure we know who we are. We live our entire lives knowing who we wanted to be when we grow up, most of the time as little girls we've already planned our wedding, we've imagined who our husband would be, and how many children we will have. As women are conditioned to believe in a fairy tale, a happily-ever-after of sorts. What I really wish I had been taught is to be who God has called me to be and to take my time. There is no rush to be one with another person. The appropriate time should be taken to become one with yourself to honestly know who you are, where you will be or want to be, and it is okay if it makes you a little bit longer than others to figure it out. You are given a model of what self-love looks like from those around you. If you cannot correctly love yourself, no one else can provide or offer love to you. You must put yourself first, know and trust God's plan for you, and when your gut tells you are with the wrong person, you must listen and move on. It is not an easy thing; it requires strength, a strength you could never imagine is inside of you if you've never had to use it.

~ *Tyeisha*

"I wish I would've never begged God for something he didn't have planned for me."

God's plan.... I'm laughing to myself because I can't count how many times I've excused behaviors and made hasty decisions and made myself believe my own choices were, in fact, "God's Plan." If you are anything like myself finding yourself praying to God for some sign about what to do next whether it be a great job opportunity, starting a business, mingling with an old friend, dating that one guy, moving across the country and even marrying your "soulmate." If we are completely honest, I think we know what we ought to do before we even ask, and maybe asking for a "sign" is a sign. God gave all of us free will to make our own individual choices. When he placed Adam and Eve in the Garden, God gave them one rule, a strict disclosure that stated, "You may freely eat any fruit in the garden except fruit from the tree of knowledge of good and evil. If you eat its fruit, you will surely die." Adam had a choice, he was not some robotic creature that had to obey, he was a man given clear direction, yet the ultimate decision was up to him. Often in life, we make decisions outside of God's will for our lives, and the only blueprint for his will is found in his Word. Just as it was written for Adam to not eat from the tree, God has also written other rules for us to follow. When it comes to life-changing decisions are, we seeking God's Word? For example, God gave us clear principles to follow when it comes to making decisions, but he won't force us to follow his word as he didn't for Adam and Eve. When we make critical decisions outside of God's will, we end up paying for them? Many of us find ourselves in dead-end jobs, toxic relationships, uncompromising marriages, and the list can go on and on. The great news in all of this is nothing that can destroy HIS will for our lives. We may go through detours, dark roads, even twisted journeys, but in the end, his grace will always save us. I've found in my storm the source of my strength; is God and his word. My advice is to stop praying for what YOU want and pray for what God has for you. Take the road less traveled, and the reward will be grand.

~ *Alicia*

"Go to therapy."

Moving in with my grandparents and them becoming my legal guardian, I had the opportunity to go to counseling. I remember my grandmother vividly discouraging me from talking with a counselor for fear I would be removed from her home, or worse institutionalized. I don't believe I fully understood what she meant. She told me to be careful with what I shared, causing me to make the decision to share nothing. I firmly believe therapy at that time would have been pivotal to who I became after leaving high school. Still not having sought counseling, after the loss of my father, experiencing heartache, failed relationships, and two children, as an adult, I understand the importance of talking with someone and getting things off your chest. Seeing a therapist allows you freedom of judgment from what you speak on, something that hold you trapped to your past, and grants you the ability to press forward. If done correctly, you receive clarity into who you are and review mental illnesses and variables that affect who you are. In my transparency, I wish I had therapy when it mattered, as I was growing and learning about myself as I embraced what the future had in store for me.

Alicia R. Stokes & Tyeisha L. Dalton

~ *Tyeisha*

"I looked for love I didn't get from my mom, now it's taking me a lifetime to heal from the choices I've made."

When asking friends and family to share comments for the book, to my surprise this was delivered by a man. Never expecting this; not because men don't have feelings nor the right to feel, simply put men are taught to be strong and never show feelings. This comment grants heavy exposure into hurt but admission acknowledges great strength. I truly and sincerely appreciate this young man's strength in sharing his stronghold. This statement holds such profound truth, we are all in pursuit of being loved and accepted. The transparency in this statement made me realize that all of us are healing from something usually stemming from childhood. Unresolved issues tend to stain our adulthood forcing us to seek after anything that can temporarily bandage the wounds we were dealt. Wounds left untreated reopen and bleed over our lives causing pain intertwined with good intentions. I've come to learn our parents are in fact imperfect people learning their way and navigating through life as we are. In a perfect world, parents would be able to love and care for their children as God loves all of us. They would ensure every single need was met and none of them was left feeling neglected, abandoned, unseen, unheard, victimized or abused. Unfortunately, sin has plagued our world as we know it and abuse, neglect, toxicity, and pain has been passed on generationally and our children are paying the price. I think of all the men who may identify with feeling unloved either by a mother or father and realize the impact this can have on a man and the families they create. Men and women coming together, procreating and looking for their partners to fill a void that only God can fulfill. In realizing that, there's no person on this earth that can make you feel whole or heal you from the things you've encountered. If you identify with this then I encourage you to practice forgiveness, there is strength in it. You owe it to yourself and to the generations coming up after you to forgive and end the lies that Satan has told you and your family for years. ~*Alicia*

"I wish I had a better example of love between a man and a woman."

Very early on for me, I knew my mother's preference was different. I was often told, "the Apple wouldn't fall far from the tree or doesn't fall far from the tree," so I never quite felt comfortable with any feeling other than a man and a woman in a relationship. This made me resentful in specific ways, especially considering my father was not there to fill in the blanks. I've come to understand that whoever and whatever you believe in is solely up to you. If you think men and women are the only dynamic that works, then I respect that. But what I have learned is that no matter the circumstance, love must be unconditional, patient, kind, and everything the Bible speaks about in 1 Corinthians 13:4-8.

Love is patient, love is kind. It does not envy, it does not boast, it is not proud. 5 It does not dishonor others, it is not self-seeking, it is not easily angered, it keeps no record of wrongs. 6 Love does not delight in evil but rejoices with the truth. 7 It always protects, always trusts, always hopes, always perseveres. 8 Love never fails. But where there are prophecies, they will cease; where there are tongues, they will be stilled; where there is knowledge, it will pass away.

~ *Tyeisha*

"Accountability is key...own it!! The Good, the Bad and the Ugly."

Accountability stings! Every lie you've grown accustomed to telling yourself begins to eat away at your soul, gradually eroding the truth that so desperately wants to set you free. There are countless books, memes, social media posts, even friends and family that continuously root and support placing the blame on everyone else except ourselves. The truth of the matter is, and yes, this might sting. You've accepted everything that has happened to you because you didn't love yourself. You didn't know what God says about you. Every lie you accepted, every toxic relationship you stayed in, every time you excused mistreatment, abuse, and infidelity is a direct result of you not loving you. All of this is such a hard pill to swallow, but no one has done anything to you as an adult that you didn't allow. I am guilty of this, and I am sure this is evident as you've turned the pages to my story.

I've excused so much toxicity and mistreatment simply because I didn't know who I was and didn't know my worth, I gave a discount after discount to be validated, loved, seen and accepted. I truly believed if I gained the merits and credentials of the people, I love would see my worth. Yet, I held 2 degrees, making very good money and still found myself in a hospital bed wanting to end my life. Many of us grow up doubting the love of God because of the failed relationships we've encountered with others. You will never know your worth or see your value until you begin to turn the pages of God's word. If you are at a point in your life where you are reflecting on your past because of the heartache, you caused yourself I urge you to own the good, the bad, and the ugly. When you love God, nothing you've endured is lost or wasted; it is merely pain draped with grace, wisdom, and favor.

~Alicia

www.ingramcontent.com/pod-product-compliance
Lightning Source LLC
Chambersburg PA
CBHW051840090426
42736CB00011B/1894